T0131683

Engaging Encounters

Inspirational Stories for Purposeful Living

Simon Aranonu

WESTBOW
P R E S S®
A DIVISION OF THOMAS NELSON
& ZONDERVAN

WestBow Press books may be ordered through booksellers or by contacting:

WestBow Press
A Division of Thomas Nelson & Zondervan
1663 Liberty Drive
Bloomington, IN 47403
www.westbowpress.com
844-714-3454

Scripture taken from the King James Version of the Bible.

ISBN: 978-1-6642-5709-2 (sc)
ISBN: 978-1-6642-5710-8 (hc)
ISBN: 978-1-6642-5711-5 (e)

Library of Congress Control Number: 2022902612

Print information available on the last page.

WestBow Press rev. date: 05/19/2022

This book is dedicated to PASTOR E.A. ADEBOYE

Contents

Preface

I've had some amazing life experiences. Through high school, university, marriage, career, ministry, and travels, my life to date has been full of stories worth telling. I've shared some of these with close friends, and many have confirmed that the stories contain life lessons that need to be shared. So I have decided to share them with a wider audience in this book.

Many years of my life have been like going through a training school. My experiences have run the gamut from amazingly beautiful to extremely challenging. As I engage in deep introspection, I realize that each of these unique encounters has been an example of providence at work to inspire or encourage someone, either now or in the future.

You are likely to read a story in this book similar to something you have either passed through or are currently experiencing. I am convinced that the answers you seek may be unveiled to you as you read. It is time for your spirit to be inspired and encouraged.

No matter your challenges, you may be surprised that countless others have faced something similar. The most important thing is not how the problems started, how long they lasted, and how people treated you in your pain, but rather whether your story ends well. The good news is that you are still alive, and so you have an opportunity to learn from other people's stories and chart a course for your own solution. There is hope, and help is available!

I welcome you to read my stories and learn their lessons. Many of these tales will make you smile, while others may make you weep for joy. Some will connect to your own untold stories and lift your spirit. It's a new dawn. Leave the painful baggage behind. Reposition and relaunch yourself. Plan a new strategy. Become optimistic. Focus on the future. A better and new you is about to emerge. I am confident that your stories will soon begin to inspire others.

—Simon Aranonu

Acknowledgments

I thank the Almighty God who has not only kept me alive to tell my stories but also given me the mental capacity to recollect events and learn lessons from them.

I feel indebted and remain ever grateful to my daddy in the Lord, Pastor E. A. Adeboye, for mentoring, encouraging, blessing, and inspiring me for the past twenty-seven years.

I am grateful to my wife, Ijeoma, for her immeasurable support and life partnership. I appreciate my children—Dumebi, Naza, Chizi, and Isaac—for always making me proud.

I am particularly appreciative of Pastor I. D. Ogufere. The idea behind writing this book was principally hers. Thank you, Pastor I. D.

My thanks go to Pastor Mrs. Modupe Olorunjo for proofreading this book.

Thank you, Pastor Mike Maduagwu, for the usual secretarial, administrative, and other logistics support.

I must confess that the success of my previous books, *Solution Capsules* and *Financial Freedom*, has inspired and encouraged me to write a third. This book is therefore coming because of positive reader support and encouraging words. You spurred me to go for another one, and here it is.

Chapter 1

Early Childhood Stories

Our first teachers in life are our parents. As we grow older, our teachers in elementary and high school complement the training received from our parents. At some point, peer groups become our unofficial teachers. We are also taught about life at our places of worship. Close relatives, older siblings, uncles, and aunties also influence us. That is how I was brought up.

These teachers help in one way or another to mold us to become what we are today. However, sometimes we forget the truths they teach us and then derail or make grievous errors. In my case, I made many mistakes despite comprehensive teachings and training. Experience, they say, is the best teacher, and I learned from my mistakes. I got better.

I believe you can also learn from my mistakes as well. Enjoy the stories.

Big Brother

I had just become a freshman in a missionary school far from my hometown. My father initially objected to my attending the boarding school because he thought I was too young to live far from home. The only reason he eventually agreed was because he heard that my older cousin was a senior student there and was confident my cousin would look after me.

Within the first month at school, I experienced some turbulent times. An experience I can't forget was when I went with some other students to get water from the motorized borehole water system. We queued with our buckets, each of us patiently waiting our turn. Out of nowhere, a young boy appeared and, ignoring the queue, walked straight up to the tap to fill his bucket. That was an insult, so I led the team that resisted him, not knowing he was sent by one of the school's senior bullies.

The young boy ran back to the hostel to report us to the bully. I had already fetched my water when the bully arrived, panting. He emptied my bucket and slapped me. I saw stars. He ordered me to lie flat on the muddy ground. While I was on the ground, he started beating the other young students. In my pain, I remembered that I had a big brother. I ran to call my cousin and told him what happened, and he followed me there.

My cousin was big and a well-respected senior. As soon as we arrived, I pointed out the bully. My cousin warned him never to touch me again. The bully backed off. I rejoiced from that day, as no senior ever tried to harass me again.

Life Lessons

1. **Never take anyone at face value.** One of the biggest mistakes I made that day was to see the young boy as just one of my classmates. I got a thorough beating because I did not know that a bully had sent him. Obviously, my attitude would have been different if I had known better.

   Behind some drivers, messengers, and security guards are influential people. You may never know until you harm them. Many people you treat badly or with disdain know people who can help you. Treat everyone well, regardless of their status or social standing. You never know!

In all honesty, if I had known the young boy had the backing of a bully, I might have stayed away from trouble. This does not excuse the bad behavior of the boy or the bully, but I advise you to be careful, as some people you encounter represent larger interests.

2. **Be humble.** If you do not humble yourself, you may be humbled. No matter how successful you are, there are people more successful than you. No matter how strong you are, someone is stronger than you. That big bully thought he was the strongest—until my big brother arrived. He was humbled.

3. **Long-term planning is required before a project.** My father knew all about bullies. He was sure I could not make it in boarding school without my cousin there to support me. He factored that into his long-term strategic planning for the survival of his little son.

   Similarly, before you start that new job, have a plan for your future. Before you attend that new school, develop a plan for your stay there. Before you go into that marriage, have a strategy for your home. Take an umbrella with you if you think it may rain. Never build a house without installing thunder arresters; lightning and thunder may strike at any time. Never drive without a spare tire; one of your tires may deflate during the journey. Provide for contingencies all the time.

4. **Don't envy those who laugh early.** That little boy laughed when the big bully arrived. But I laughed when my cousin arrived. The little boy laughed early; I laughed last. It is not those who laugh at the beginning who are guaranteed to laugh last. Don't mock those who have not yet made it in life. Some don't make it early but succeed in middle age or

the evening of their lives. The world is often like a game of musical chairs. You never know. Only God knows.

My Village Bicycle

My village bicycle, a Raleigh, actually belonged to my mother. She was a seamstress who worked hard to acquire it. Her mother had blessed her with a hand-powered sewing machine as a wedding gift. Given the poverty level in the rural areas in those days, people hardly bought new clothes. They just kept mending their old clothes over and over until the fabric gave way. My mother was particularly good at patching, and the villagers kept coming back to her. She would often fortify the torn portion of her customers' clothes with a brand-new piece of cloth and strengthen the weak areas. Occasionally, new clothes were sewn, but mainly as uniforms for schoolchildren and during festive periods like Christmas.

Soon, my mother's income was decent enough to buy a brand-new bicycle. Her father assisted her in buying it, and it was indeed a sight to behold. Villagers who needed to go on long-distance trips would occasionally ask to borrow it. In our village at the time, no one owned a car or motorbike, so bicycle owners were highly respected.

This was an adult bicycle, so the height could not be adjusted for children. As a young boy of nine, I was not tall enough to sit and cycle, but I managed to ride it nonetheless.

The village market, held every four days, was where people sold their goods, including various foodstuffs and hardware. Most families bought foodstuffs that would last the four days. There was no electricity or refrigeration, so fish, for example, was preserved by roasting. My mother attended this village market religiously, even though it was five kilometers away.

My job on market days was to use the bicycle to carry my mother's sewing machine and patched-up clothes to the market, where she would deliver them to their owners. I would drop the clothes off at the house of a relative who lived a three-minute walk from the market so my mother could pick them up from there, and then I would walk the seven kilometers to school. In the evening, I would return from school, stop at our relative's house, pick up the sewing machine and a new load of torn clothes requiring patching, and ride my mother's bicycle home. This routine lasted for years.

When I graduated from university, the first major asset I acquired was a bicycle. I started riding out of necessity, but to this day, I still love bicycles. I taught all my children how to ride. Very few people know the history behind my love for bicycles.

Life Lessons

1. **Hard work pays.** I have yet to find an alternative to hard work. My mother taught me hard work and how to juggle many balls at the same time without dropping any. She was a tailor, a farmer, and a trader. She inculcated that spirit in me. Her hard work distinguished her in the village. That brand-new Raleigh bicycle made us stand out, but it was the fruit of hard work.

2. **Foundations can influence tomorrow.** I learned to ride a bicycle to help my mum. It became the first real "machine" I learned to use in life. Today, my key hobby is bicycle-riding. It gives me great joy. At the same time, it has been the main way I have stayed fit for the last forty years. When I cannot ride outdoors, I ride a stationary bicycle.

3. **There is nothing wrong with repairs.** Watching my mother patch those torn clothes taught me the virtue of maintenance. Nothing should be thrown away if it can be repaired or mended.

4. **Your skill makes you stand out.** My mother's skill as a trained seamstress made her stand out in the village market,

and people trusted her. She patched loads of used clothes and made money from it. This contributed significantly to our upkeep at home.

5. **Use equipment in multiple ways.** My mother's bicycle was used for her business and for my pleasure. It was also useful for relatives and friends who regularly borrowed it for long-distance journeys. Today, many people own cars that can be rented or used through Uber or Lyft to make additional income. Be wise, and let your assets produce multiple streams of income.

My Oversized School Shoes

After graduating from the village elementary school, I secured admission into a high boarding school. My dad was facing huge financial challenges at the time. Following pressure from one of my older cousins, however, my father agreed to pay my way. Beyond tuition and boarding fees, I also needed uniforms, mosquito nets, cutlery, suitcases, and so on. Daddy did his best to buy all those, except for one that had a surprise attached to it.

The surprise was the official school shoes. They were called Cortina shoes and were sold by a foreign company. Because the shoes were expensive, there was a cheaper local version being sold for less than 50 percent of the price. My father went for the local version for his lovely son. That was what he could afford. May God bless his soul.

But there was a bigger surprise. Daddy bought the wrong size; the shoes were much too big for me, and I was sure he had made a mistake. When I complained, he sat me down and explained that he had deliberately bought the larger size so they would last longer. He advised me to stuff the shoes with old newspapers, and they would be more comfortable when my feet grew into the shoe size.

It was a great chat, and he took time to provide insight about his financial challenges and the need to manage. Initially, I was distraught, but then I calmed down, and off to school I went.

When I arrived at the school, my self-esteem immediately came under attack. My fellow students mocked me daily for both the local version of the shoes and their large size. But, remembering my dad's explanation, I refused to be bullied. I was there for studying, not a fashion show. I faced my studies with zeal and commitment. After all, there was no connection between my shoes and my brain.

By the grace of God, I used those shoes for the first four years of secondary school. I did well. I became a house prefect and a strong leader without feeling inferior or subordinate. I eventually graduated with excellent grades, and now I can buy whatever shoes I want.

Life Lessons

1. **Children have the capacity to learn if you teach them.** My father's explanation of his financial state helped me manage mockery from peers. When you pass through challenging times, please explain that to your children, no matter how young they are. It will keep them from becoming resentful or rebellious.

2. **There is always a less-expensive alternative.** If you can't afford designer clothes, buy something affordable. If you can't afford a five-star airline for your trip, choose a budget carrier. If you can't afford a first-class ticket, buy an economy ticket. If you can't afford a holiday in the south of France, visit the south of your country. If you can't afford a beautiful meal in an upscale restaurant, visit a local one or cook at home. If you can't afford a Mercedes-Benz or BMW, buy a Korean-made car or a used Toyota, or use public transportation. Sooner than you can imagine, that phase will pass, and you will upgrade.

3. **Don't let other people's opinion shape your destiny.** I'm grateful I was strong on the inside. My fellow students did not defeat me mentally. I held on strong. None of them knew my family history. Only he who wears the shoe knows where it pinches. Bad friends aggravate pain by reiterating the fact that the shoe pinches! You need friends who will encourage you, not fault-finders or mockers.

Trained Witch Doctor

I came to high school very green, naïve, and timid, just in from a village elementary school. Barely a month after my arrival, our school was to play an important football match against another school. The match was crucial to move to local government and state championships.

Our school seniors were determined to win that game at all costs—so determined, they decided to seek supernatural powers and visited a local witch doctor who claimed to be formidable and foreign-trained. The witch doctor demanded money, so they returned to the hostel and, at midnight, went round the dormitories waking us up one by one, demanding that we contribute to the special fund. We had no choice but to donate from our meagre allowance, under the intimidating eyes of the seniors.

As a result, we were sure of victory. The witch doctor's charm would certainly ensure that we trashed the opposition. All we had to do was obey the witch doctor's specific instructions: our goalkeeper should run to the opposition's goalpost and dance a little immediately after the referee blew the whistle signaling the beginning of the game. Thereafter, he was to run back to his post. To our dismay, however, the opposition would not let him near their post and chased him away.

That game was a disaster for our team; we were thoroughly

beaten. We cried all night and refused dinner. That event left me with some lessons that have shaped my life to date.

Life Lessons

1. **Children are vulnerable to manipulation.** Seniors were of great influence back then, and we believed everything they told us. Parents need to watch their children closely. Many children are molested in boarding schools. A lot of evil habits are learned in schools, and false ideologies may be picked up. Watch out for unusual behavior when students return home for holidays. A stitch in time saves nine.

2. **There is no shortcut to success.** Our seniors tried to use a powerless charm to achieve success, but success requires skill and hard work. If you don't work hard, failure is guaranteed. In life, only the diligent can be successful. Hard work is indispensable for success.

3. **You need God to bless your work.** We went to the wrong place to seek help. The devil cannot help you succeed or achieve victory. It is God who gives victory. Ask God to bless the work of your hands. When God blesses the work of your hands, success is guaranteed.

4. **Many bad things are "cooked" in the night.** Those seniors came to us at midnight. Why was this plan not announced in the morning or at evening assembly? Why did they hide it from the teachers? The seniors obviously knew what they were doing was wrong.

   Watch out for activities that take place under the cover of darkness and behind closed doors. Nobody commits adultery openly. Thieves operate undercover. Holy meetings are held in the open. The way of the wicked is darkness. Be careful with meetings held under the cover of darkness.

5. **Dealing with deceivers ultimately ends in sorrow.** We contributed money and were hopeful, but it turned to sorrow at the end of the game. Nobody can give you what he or she does not have. The witch doctor took our pocket money and our joy, and destroyed our football team. Only God can bless without sorrow.

Finally, note that deceivers are sly and crafty. The witch doctor deceived our seniors, who in turn deceived us. We could not even ask for a refund. You will succeed if you seek God's blessings.

Beautiful Nonsense

In some years past, a lot of the beer consumed in my country was imported from Europe. It was handy, canned in fifty-centiliter sizes, and attractively packaged in transparent cartons of twenty-four per pack. I was a teenager then and had never tasted beer. I loved the unique taste of Coca-Cola, the sparkle of Sprite, the sweetness of Fanta, and the maturity of nonalcoholic malt drinks.

I often saw adults excitedly boasting about how many cans of beer they could consume. Beer was a major means of entertaining guests while chatting for long hours. Beer parlors sprang up all over town, filled with adults who would enjoy the beer along with freshly prepared meat delicacies. Naturally, as a teenager I was inquisitive. I wanted to understand why adults preferred beer to my sweet Fanta. I just could not wait to join the adult club to find out.

Then came Christmas. My father bought a few cartons of beer to celebrate. I smuggled a can into my room, shut the door, quietly opened it, and took a sip. To my horror, it was bitter—nothing to compare with my sweet Fanta. I was determined to finish it, though, hoping it might become sweeter as I drank more. Nothing changed. It was bitter all the way. To say that I was disappointed was an understatement.

But that's not the whole story. Barely thirty minutes afterward, I started feeling dizzy. I lay down hoping I would soon be OK, but I felt worse. The ceiling turned round and round, and I started hallucinating! It was an hour before I returned to normal. I'm glad my father did not knock on my door. I've kept this secret for forty-two years.

That was the beginning of the end of my journey with beer. I've had a few more bottles since, but my experience has never been good. I am glad to say goodbye to alcoholic drinks. It's been over thirty years since I've tasted any.

Life Lessons

1. **Curiosity kills the cat.** Teenagers are curious by nature, and they will often do anything to satisfy their curiosity. Accordingly, teenagers need close monitoring. Our current "e-world" is more challenging than the world I grew up in. Access to the internet makes it difficult to monitor young people. That's why we hear of cyberbullying and dangerous substance abuse leading to the premature death of many young people. It's sad that some young people end up in psychiatric hospitals because of such practices. Child prostitution can arise from such exposure when there is no monitoring. Nobody knew what transpired in my room that day. If I had continued, it would certainly have been a problem.

2. **Labels may differ from content.** The label and packaging of that beer was attractive. Adults appeared to enjoy it. Advertising of the product on television made it even more inviting. However, the taste was bitter. It did not meet my expectations.

   In life, many things are like beer. You cannot vouch for anything until you test it personally. In marriage, you can't vouch for a potential spouse until you get married because some pretense happens during courtship. The real person can be known only when you live together. That's why you need divine direction to choose a life partner.

Practically every product you want to purchase will be beautifully packaged, including real estate, clothing, educational institutions, and even medicine. As they say, "The taste of the pudding is in the eating." Don't be carried away by external attributes that fade as soon as you unwrap the product. Be concerned about the content, which is the reality.

3. **We are all differently configured.** One can of beer sent me into the world of hallucinations. But some of my friends could drink three cans of beer and suffer no side effects. This reminds me of a madman I used to see on the streets. I was told he sniffed a little bit of a dangerous drug and became instantly mad. However, some of his classmates who did the same suffered no such effects. We are all different. Please do not copy others; be yourself. Don't do anything just because others are doing it. We're all different.

Black Coffee and Biology

We were writing our last internal examinations in high school, called mock exams. It was a rehearsal to prepare us for the main external examinations just before our West African School Certificate Exams (WASC). We therefore took it seriously.

Biology was not one of my favorite subjects, and I was scared on the eve of the biology mock exam. Ordinarily, I loved to score above 90 percent in every subject, and I worked hard to achieve that, but biology was always a drag on my grades.

Then one of my classmates shared a secret with me on the

eve of the exam. He told me he took black coffee in the evening, and that helped him stay awake all night to study and then excel. I bought the idea and drank coffee generously. It worked: I stayed awake and started studying. And that's where the good news ended.

By two in the morning, everyone in the house was fast asleep, and I was wide awake. I wanted to study more, but my head was pounding. At three in the morning, I crawled into my bunkbed, hoping to sleep. Yet my eyes remained wide open. I prayed to fall asleep, but I could not. I remained awake until six in the morning.

When I got to the exam hall, my head was still pounding. I faced the exam with apparent seriousness but couldn't remember anything. It was the most disastrous examination of my life. I ended up with a score of 22 percent.

That was the last time I ever drank black coffee.

Life Lessons

1. **One man's food is another man's poison.** Black coffee worked for my friend, yet it wrought havoc on me. Find out what works for you. It may not necessarily be what works for another person. We are all different. Take time to know yourself. You are unique. You will enjoy life if you know yourself.

   My wife likes variety and keeps recreating her environment. That's how she's wired. I'm different. Unless she calls on me to order another, I can wear the same pair of shoes for ten years. That's me.

   Do not copy someone else. Know yourself and your purpose. Know the resources you need to achieve your purpose. Go ahead and do what makes you happy if it aligns with your purpose and is moral and legal.

2. **Avoid last-minute trials.** The greatest mistake I made on that day was to try out coffee the night before the

examination. That was risky and dangerous. It would have been better for that experiment to have taken place days or even weeks before the exam. If I had done it much earlier, I would have done better on my exam. My advice to you is not to take last-minute risks. If you want to try something new, do not try it, for example, on the eve of your wedding. Any experiment on the eve of a major event could be potentially disastrous.

3. **Preparation has no substitute.** I was unprepared for that exam. I knew I had not studied enough and felt I needed emergency all-night study. The problem was that I had not prepared well enough before that, so I started looking for shortcuts. I thought the all-night idea would do it, but there is no shortcut to success. You must pay the price. It may take you many days and nights, but remember, success is not a one-night crash program.

Most people today have lost the stamina to prepare long for success. They want it like fast food. Many have a microwave mentality. They want to avoid labor and still get results. Yet success in anything in life requires months of study and preparation. Learn to prepare well ahead. Rehearse repeatedly. Stars are not made overnight. Patience and preparation are indispensable requirements for enduring success.

My Teacher's Tippex

I was about to graduate from high school, and my next focus was university. My semi-urban missionary high school was largely a science school. I was doing average in sciences but very well in commercial subjects and arts. I had just completed my University Joint Admissions form, and my first choice for course of study was medicine. My second choice was pharmacy.

Now, I had a friend called Peter. He was a friend to many teachers, being an exceptionally brilliant young man. Naturally, the teachers loved him.

One evening, Peter was on his way to visit one of our teachers, and I tagged along. As soon as we sat in the teacher's small living room, he inquired about our choice of courses for university. Peter had applied for medicine too. The teacher approved of Peter's choice but disapproved of mine. He reeled off many reasons why and instead recommended finance and accountancy as my first and second choice. I told him it was too late, since I had completed the forms. He insisted I bring the forms to him.

I ran to my hostel and brought the forms. My teacher reached out for his Tippex correction fluid, deleted my choices, and replaced them with finance and accountancy. That was how I started my journey in the world of banking and business. You might not be reading this book, and many of you would never have met me in life, if not for my teacher's Tippex.

Life Lessons

1. **It's always good to have a mentor.** That teacher was an unsolicited but God-sent mentor. Your mentors should know more than you and should be able to guide you.
2. **Your friends can help shape your destiny.** My friend Peter provided me with the privilege of visiting the teacher's residence. You need to carefully choose friends who will add value to your life. Friends will never leave you without an impact, so appraise your relationships. It's about your destiny.
3. **Young people need to be coached.** Please coach your children and wards, and their friends. I wanted to study medicine because of the honor and respect accorded to doctors. Everyone around me was applying for either

medicine or engineering. Back then, our classmates laughed at anyone who applied for non-sciences. Those students were seen as not being intelligent enough. But then, I would have been a disastrous doctor. I wouldn't have had the patience to sit down for hours daily listening to patients' complaints.

4. **There is a God factor in destiny.** Before you were born, God decided your destiny. If you cooperate with God, he will help you discover it. It could appear accidental, like my Tippex story, but believe me, it was a heavenly setup. I had an option not to accept the counsel from the teacher, but I did. You therefore must cooperate with God when He sends your own teacher with Tippex.

Many people are unfulfilled in life because they are not doing what they are configured to do. Every time they wake up to go to work, they sigh. A lady I know spent seven years in medical school. She became a doctor but never practiced medicine. She now makes cakes and says that is her calling. When I consider how God has elevated me in my profession, I can never forget my teacher's Tippex. God bless that teacher, wherever he is.

Village Standards, Global Competition

I grew up in a village and attended the village elementary school, where each year I turned out to be the best in my class. I won several prizes at each year-end prize-giving day. I remember being invited to teach elementary five pupils while I was in elementary four. The headmasters loved to show me off.

All through elementary school, I made valedictory speeches to the pupils and teachers to close the session. The beauty of my village intelligence and excellence was such that I never seriously studied, yet I remained the best. I believed I was a genius.

Then I enrolled in a first-class semi-urban high school set up by the missionaries. I continued my usual approach to academics: no serious studies and no need to do homework, since I was a genius. After the end-of-first-term exams, my position was twenty-eighth out of forty students! I recollect my father saying that the result could not be mine.

At the end of the second term, I managed to be twenty-second out of forty. My best result at the end of year one was eighteenth out of forty. My ego was deflated. Now that I was competing with the best, I realized I was not so smart. The more I studied, the more these smarter guys studied too. I never made the best four throughout my secondary school. I graduated but certainly was somewhere after the top five.

Life Lessons

1. **In the land of the blind, the one-eyed man is king.** Village standards are no equivalent to global standards. You can never say you are good until you compete on the global stage. And this applies to every facet of life. Professional footballers can't claim they are the best soccer player in the world until they leave their native country and compete with the best players in the best clubs in the world.

   The Redeemed Christian Church of God, where I am privileged to function as a pastor, was a Nigerian church from 1952 to 1980. Up until 1980, it had no branches outside Nigeria. When Pastor E. A. Adeboye became the general overseer in 1981, the quest to reach the world started. Today, it is said to be the largest evangelical church in the world, with branches in 195 nations and nearly 40,000 worship locations.

2. **The world is your territory.** It's a global village. All your services and products must meet and possibly exceed global

standards. If you are running a supermarket, look through your window; there's another one a few meters away. Amazon is now making deliveries globally. Macy's and all the world's superstores deliver to your doorstep. Unless people upgrade to global standards, they may soon eat the humble pie I ate many years ago.

Consider this: Africa's richest man is a Nigerian, and *Forbes* adjudges him to be worth about $5 billion. A few years ago, he was the richest Nigerian but not Africa's richest man. Then he began to manufacture world-class cement and set up cement plants all over Africa.

Successful internet-based companies like Twitter, Facebook, and Google provide services to global customers. Their owners are billionaires.

Long-term sustainability depends on your capacity to compete with the rest of the world. Work on upgrading your education to world-class and do the same for your children. If you are running a business, make world-class products.

Learn a lesson from me. Do not suffer the shame and humbling I passed through. Do not confuse local standards with global standards. Keep improving, even if you are already the best. Do not consider your past achievements as anything worth thinking about. Strive to beat your previous best. Do not consider yourself to have achieved anything, but keep pressing forward toward the high calling of the prize. The world is ready for you. Are you ready for the world?

The Headmaster and the Key

I was appointed school monitor by the headmaster in my community elementary school. My duties included arriving early before other pupils and teachers to open the school door. I was always the last to leave school because I also had the duty of locking the doors. This meant I went home with the school key.

One day after school, I went playing like any other child of my age. We were playing in a sandy area, and after the games, I couldn't find the school key. It had obviously fallen out of my pocket into the sand and got buried there.

I went straight to the headmaster's house to report the matter. I expected a reprieve but was shocked when he asked me to go to the market in the nearest village, buy a new padlock, and ensure a carpenter changed the lock that same evening. He gave me no money and blamed me for being careless.

I cried all the way home, where I narrated my ordeal to my mum. She gave me the money, and off I went to the local market. No shops had padlocks. I was directed to a nearby town market and walked lonely pathways on a journey of about two kilometers. As a nine-year-old, instead of walking, I naturally ran all the way. I bought the padlock, got a carpenter, and replaced the school lock.

Life Lessons

1. **Leadership can be a burden.** That incident happened over fifty years ago, but it shaped me to be more careful in life and to understand the burden of leadership and responsibility. You may think that my headmaster was mean. I thought so then too, but as I grew up, I became grateful to him.

2. **Children learn a lot early in life.** I never lost any keys after that day. If the headmaster had punished me but then replaced the lock himself, as I had hoped, I would have forgotten the corporal punishment within days. My advice is that you must teach your children lifelong lessons when they misbehave. Instead of scolding them,

consider punishments that will make them think. Take away privileges for a while.

3. **Children are smart.** Sometimes they try a few pranks to see if they can get away with it. But they need to be taught responsibility, like my headmaster taught me. We should reprimand them because we love them. If we train up a child in the way he should go, then when he is grown, he will not depart from it. Whatever lessons you learned from your own headmaster or parents, please use them to bring up your own child/ward. This way, our children will grow up responsibly.

Speaking for Someone

I was barely twelve years old, timid, and largely naïve when I completed my elementary education. My parents were poor. My father was a petty trader and my mother a seamstress.

At this time, my father arranged for my uncle to come to the village and take me to Lagos so I could become his apprentice trader. It was not my father's choice, but he knew he couldn't afford my fees for high school. My uncle arrived as agreed to take his apprentice trader to Lagos, but it was not to be.

I remember sitting outside that day, beside the window of my father's room, and seeing three village headmasters come to see my father separately but in quick succession. They each came to ask about my secondary education. I overheard my father tell each one that he would have loved for me to attend high school, but he could not afford the fees. They tried to persuade him otherwise, but his answer was always the same. He could not afford the fees.

However, the next day, my uncle returned to Lagos disappointed that he could not get his apprentice. Nobody told me what was happening, and I was too frightened to ask my father. All I knew was what I'd heard eavesdropping by my dad's window.

A week later, my father asked me to prepare to attend high school. I could not understand the sudden turn of events. I could tell it was extremely tough and financially challenging for him. But I attended and graduated from high school nonetheless.

Only three years ago, I had a deep conversation with the person who spoke on my behalf and convinced my dad to do all he could to send me to high school. That angel is my father's niece and my first cousin. She turned eighty-five this year. My father loved her so much that he could not say no to her.

Many people achieve their destinies because someone speaks on their behalf. Many destinies have also been truncated because someone spoke against them at a critical moment. Some people have been hired in destiny-fulfilling jobs because someone said something nice about them to would-be employers. Some people are not married today because a potential spouse received negative feedback about them or their family.

Today, as I sit on the boards of corporations, I insist that the truth be told about employees. I willingly lend a helping voice to staff who have no one to speak for them. When I sit on the church pastorate council, I speak for those who cannot speak for themselves, conscious of the fact that someone spoke for me too when I could not speak for myself.

Life Lessons

Every privileged position comes with responsibilities, including fairness and speaking for others. There is power in your words. You can use them to mold lives or destroy lives. Life and death are in the power of the tongue. Use your tongue to help humanity, to build and not to tear down. Do not speak out of malice. Bless people. Do not curse. Pray that God will change your enemies. Keep loving, doing well, and building lives with your words.

"You Are a Lilliputian"

One day, we were in biology class in high school. I was fourteen. Suddenly, the teacher called out my name and asked that I stand up. I obeyed, and he began to rain curses on me, calling me a *Lilliputian*. That was the first time I had heard that word. He continued with several other curses. He said I would never be useful in life.

This was a man who was possibly in his mid-thirties, cursing a young fourteen-year-old. Finally, he asked me to leave his class. I was in tears. After class, my friends asked me what I did wrong. I could not answer because I didn't know.

It took over a year for me to find out what I did. A casual friend once asked me to join him to visit a teacher who was his father's friend. It turned out to be the biology teacher. We knocked on the door. The teacher was home but had a female teacher with him and therefore didn't open the door. We could overhear her voice in the house.

My friend was disappointed and abused the teacher under his breath, calling him a flirt and a womanizer. To be honest, I joined him in saying those things. We were young students and spoke what was on our minds.

I later found out that my friend told the teacher what I said without mentioning that he started it all. That was why the teacher cursed and abused me.

Life Lessons

1. **Walls have ears.** Don't speak evil of people. There is nothing hidden that will not be exposed. Two young boys appeared to be chatting innocently. It later became a broadcast. I regret what I said, but I also learned from the incident.

2. **Never trust easily.** I trusted my friend, and he betrayed me. I ended my friendship with him when I found out what happened. But I had been terribly hurt and damaged, and that incident made me lose interest in biology.

   In life, you have to be careful. When you meet people, study them before you let your guard down. It's difficult to find people you can trust. Make many friends, but don't trust everyone. Trust only a few after they have been time-tested.

3. **Put the past behind you and move forward.** The curses from that biology teacher didn't work. When I see how far God has taken me, I know the man's curses had no effect on my destiny. I was embarrassed and emotionally abused, but I was not distracted. It made me stronger. Of course, I lost interest in biology that year, but I recovered in subsequent years when the teacher was changed.

   My advice is to ignore negative statements people make about you. Do not lose your self-esteem. Become stronger. Move on with your life. Keep working hard. Men and women can say whatever they want about you. If you are focused and hardworking, you will be on your way to the top.

4. **Mind where you visit.** The journey I made outside the school to the teacher's house was unwarranted and unnecessary. Apparently, the teacher wasn't even expecting the student I went with. If I had not made that trip, I would not have talked along the way.

5. **Learn to say no when necessary.** You don't have to accept every invitation. Your capacity to grow and succeed in life will depend a lot on your ability to turn down some invitations. Choose where you go. Some trips are completely irrelevant and unnecessary, and do not add value to our lives. Learn to decline such trips.

High School Junior Miler

In the early seventies, we measured distance in miles, and those who could run long-distance races were called *milers*. I was very young, had just enrolled in high school, and was in boarding school. There was a major sports competition coming up at the state level. Our school had a senior student who was an award-winning miler. He practiced every evening by running round the school football field several times.

One evening, I was motivated to join him in a practice race. Surprisingly, I caught up with him and overtook him. I seemed to have greater stamina and faster speed. Before long, a large crowd of students gathered to applaud me. Soon, my name was changed to Junior Miler, and there was a belief that a new long-distance-race runner had been born. I felt on top of the world.

Three weeks later, our school organized an inter-house sports competition. All eyes were on me to win the long-distance race, and my hall of residence was very hopeful of a gold medal. This time, however, the long-distance race would not be on the pitch but through the town and along several roads. Contrary to expectations, my run was a disaster. The mature award-winning miler took the gold. Some unknown runners received silver and bronze medals. I came in at the forty-first position. It was a monumental disaster for me, and a rude shock.

Life Lessons

1. **Rehearsal is not the main event.** When the experienced champion was practicing, we all thought he was at his best. But I overtook him one evening and began to think too highly of myself. For him, it was just a practice session. On the day of the competition, his performance was clearly different.

It's like courtship. There is no guarantee that the marriage will be exactly like the courtship. The same applies to examinations. Some students excel at mock examinations but fail at the real examination. You cannot judge or appraise others until they really participate at the championship. Preparatory activities do not guarantee success at main events.

2. **Champions are made from repeated practice.** That champion practiced every evening at the school football pitch. I only practiced once and outran him. I didn't know that a person needs daily practice sessions to excel.

   Life is exactly like that. Anything you want to achieve must cost you intense, long practice sessions. Nobody will ever become a champion without working hard over a long period. Hard work has no alternative. Many want to gate-crash into success, but it doesn't happen that way. Before a boxer picks up a championship belt, he practices for many months. Get ready to work hard over the long haul if you want to be celebrated at the top.

3. **Pride comes before a fall.** I confess that I was proud before that competition. When I ran past that champion at the football pitch, I felt I was the new champion. When I was nicknamed Junior Miler, I believed I was the next big thing in town. I felt important, with a chip on my shoulder and an inflated ego. I went into that race believing I would win. My friends also gave me a false impression of myself.

   Pride always precedes a fall. You must be humble to get to the top. Humility makes you respect the talents and skills of others while ensuring you prepare well, knowing others have prepared too. Humility compels you to avoid underestimating the opposition, while pride makes you underprepare and underperform. Never go into a competition believing that you are the smartest. Those who think that way will always fall behind.

4. **Do your research.** I didn't know the competition would be held in the town, with its mountains and valleys. That took me by surprise. I thought it would be held on the school pitch. Students who knew the location were ready. They had the right footwear. They arranged for hydration and had practice sessions along the same pathways. I was just very naïve and not prepared for such a major event.

In life, I encourage you to always seek out information before engaging in any contest. Knowledge will set you apart. You need to know about your opponents, the environment, and the rules. Life is all about competition. There is competition in business, academic studies, and politics. We fight spiritual battles with the devil. In whatever contest you enter, please ensure you are sufficiently empowered with knowledge and relevant information.

Chapter 2

Campus Stories

When I enrolled in university, I felt I was old enough to make decisions for myself, was responsible for my actions as a legal adult, and knew enough to live my own life. I relished my newfound freedom. All I wanted was to live alone, far from parental control, and enjoy my life.

However, I was also naïve, ignorant, and without a mentor. Consequently, I made mistakes. Some could have left me with a devastating untold impact, but somehow, help came.

Welcome to life on campus. My stories are captivating and full of lessons.

Undergraduate Foolishness

Attending a rural elementary and high school limited my exposure and vision. I lacked basic wisdom. My travel had been limited, and I had not been exposed to any form of sophistication. Meanwhile, many of my colleagues had been on summer vacations overseas. Many had attended federal government or Kings/Queens colleges. I was intimidated by their credentials and their amazing phonetics. My self-esteem was shaken.

In addition to all these deficiencies, I knew little or nothing about university education, as I was the first university graduate from my family. For me, a university degree was my passport to getting a good job. But I knew nothing about graduation grades like first class or second class. And so, at the end of my first year, I ended up with an average performance that was close to a third-class degree. My university's grading system was such that results of the first three years would give a 50 percent score, while the final year would determine another 50 percent. Both put together would determine the final grade.

After my first year, I met a good friend who I will call UB (not his real name). His sister worked in the Central Bank and had advised him to strive to make a first-class or, at the minimum, a second-class upper grade. That would make him stand out in the job market and ensure he got a good job after graduation. UB was on track to a second-class upper in the first year, and he encouraged me to buckle up so that we could graduate together with top grades. That advice changed my life.

I fired on all cylinders academically, graduated with a second-class upper degree, and became an awardee of the university's foundation prize as the best graduating student in the class. My joy is that UB also graduated with a second-class upper degree.

Life Lessons

1. **Never lose your self-esteem .** I was intimidated by the background of the other students. To be honest, they had an edge over me, with many of them having attended A-levels. They were smart, with a beautiful pedigree. This nearly ruined my first year on campus.

   When we got to the second year, I saw the initial advantage they had over me fizzle out. Everything depended on how much personal study and research I did. My self-esteem was back, and it kept surging until we graduated. All the students who made me feel intimidated in the first year were still there when I graduated top-of-the-class. Never lose your confidence or self-esteem.

2. **Make good friends.** I'm happy I met my friend UB. We were the same age, but he was much wiser and more experienced. He had educated relatives, which I didn't have. My friendship with UB changed the course of my life for the better.

   Who are your friends? You must make friends with people who are smarter and wiser than you are if you want to excel in life. It is important that your friends have an ambition to excel, good moral values, and a vision for their life.

   Choose your friends wisely. Do not let your friends choose you. If a friend is not adding value to your life, you need to drop that person. Stop wasting time with time-wasters.

3. **Your past does not determine your future.** I attended poorly funded rural schools. My parents were poor and not educated. But none of this stopped me. Nothing is impossible. When you make up your mind to be the best, God will back you up. But you have your part to play, and you must work hard and study hard. Burn the midnight candle if you must and don't be distracted.

   One of the first actions I took after UB's counsel was to resign from the socio-cultural club I had joined on campus. I needed to focus on one singular issue, which was creating a new foundation, and God helped me. Forget your poor inadequate upbringing and disadvantages. With hard work, holiness, and humility, you can't be stopped from getting to the top.

Freshman, Fresh Favor

I traveled several kilometers to the city of Enugu to enroll as a freshman at University of Nigeria for a degree in finance. When I arrived that morning, I went to the admissions office and joined the registration queue. We had to provide relevant documentation, which the registration officials would scrutinize before registering us. Successful registration provided a guarantee of accommodation on campus.

The students lined up at four registration points, but the process was cumbersome and painfully slow. Registration of each student took about twenty-five minutes, and we could see that the process was bound to take several days. As we waited, I started chatting with the guy behind me. We became friends and realized we had a lot in common. Our friendship helped to alleviate some of our frustration from having to wait in line.

We were on the queue from about ten in the morning until three in the afternoon. Suddenly, there was an announcement that the registration counters would be closing and would continue the next day. Our major worry was where we would sleep that night.

When this announcement was made, there were ten people ahead of me, and from my calculation, the lady officer could only attend to one more person. She attended to him. Then she broke protocol and decided to attend to one more person. She pointed to me, and I ran forward.

She registered me, and a room was immediately allocated to me. It was room B11 in Samuel Manuwa Hall, and since my new friend had no room to sleep in, I decided to share it with him. His name was Odilibe. Our friendship was further solidified as we talked all through the night. We discovered that we were pursuing the same degree in finance. He was a Lagos boy from a rich home. I was a village boy from poor parents. Yet we loved each other.

Two relationships started on that first day of registration. The first was with Odilibe, who became my bosom friend, confidant, counselor, soulmate, and intimate friend for the next twenty years. He was smart, wise, humble, and an entrepreneur at heart. I learned a lot from him. Our friendship extended to our families. Very sadly, Odilibe has passed on, but I still love and miss him. I'll never find another friend like him.

The second relationship that started that first day was with Mrs. K, the elderly woman who sought me out in the large crowd to register me ahead of my classmates. I later got to know that she was a campus accountant and the assistant bursar. I reciprocated her kind gesture by visiting her office regularly. Soon I had a mother on the campus, and she had a new son. Throughout my four years on campus, I would visit her for meals or soft drinks any time I ran out of money. I would love to meet any of Mrs. K's children one day to extend appreciation to them for their mother's sake.

Life Lessons

1. **Favor makes you stand out.** Why did Mrs. K point at me even though I was in the middle of the queue? Some will call it luck; I call it divine favor that will make men break protocol to bless you, single you out in the crowd, and distinguish you. It will make you first among equals. I pray that God will give you favor from today.

2. **One good turn deserves another.** I could have thanked Mrs. K and moved on. But I nurtured the relationship. I kept visiting her. She accepted me as her son. That relationship blessed me greatly on campus. When I returned to campus a few years later, I went looking for her to reward her. Unfortunately, I was told she had retired and returned to her hometown. There were no cell phones in those days. I could not re-establish that relationship.

    Today, there are many fair-weather friends who stay

close only if they can benefit from you. Unfortunately, such relationships have no meaning and do not endure. The relationships you nurture despite what you may gain or lose will pay you in the long run. Your best friends are those who have been with you through thick and thin, and loved you while you were in high school or university. Nurture such friends. They are the ones who love you for who you are, not for what you have.

3. **There are no accidental meetings.** Why was Odilibe right behind me on the queue that day? Why did he not secure a room that day but had to sleep in my room? How come my first friend in the university was also my course mate? Some may call it a coincidence, but I call it a divine setup, or destiny at work.

Everyone you meet has a purpose arranged by God. You may not know it now. Offering my room to Odilibe opened a lifetime of a mutually beneficial relationship. Every time someone is in need, do not hesitate to help if you can. That little relationship that started that day was extended to all members of my family.

Be nice to people. Put up a cheerful face. Help people who come your way. Like the elders say: tomorrow is pregnant, and nobody knows what it will deliver. Anything can happen in the future. The person you respect and honor today can become the governor in ten years' time. Keep doing good works.

All We Are Saying Is, Give Us Water

I was a teenager and had just become a freshman at the university. I had quickly made a friend on campus. He was a nice cool guy who always listened to my advice.

Barely a week after classes started, the campus water system broke down, and we had to go in search of water daily outside the campus. Soon enough, some students organized themselves to demonstrate against the university authorities, especially the deputy vice chancellor (DVC), who was the de facto CEO of the campus.

The demonstration was massive. It was exciting and appealed particularly to freshmen like us who had never experienced such a thing before. The organizers made it fun. They made a small wooden coffin for the DVC and marched around campus with pallbearers carrying the coffin and occasionally stopping to weep. At the DVC's house, we chorused a made-up song: "All we are saying is, give us water." Imagine the audacity! But I had the fun of my life along with my friend.

The following day, many of the demonstrators were invited to face a disciplinary committee, while others received suspension letters. My friend and I panicked for days on end. We prayed that we would be safe, and miraculously, we escaped by providence.

What we did not know was that throughout the demonstration, there were fifth columnists among us who were busy writing down the names of the demonstrators.

Life Lessons

1. **Your friends may not always be right.** Friends are sometimes honestly and sincerely wrong. I invited my friend to a demonstration that almost landed him in trouble. Weigh all pieces of critical advice from friends.

2. **Life is filled with fifth columnists.** In every group action, you are likely to find them. Be conscious of that. The heart of men is desperately wicked. Who can know it? You will always find bad guys among apparently good people with a noble objective.

3. **Do not follow others to do evil.** I followed others to demonstrate. I went scot-free, but many others got into trouble. I enjoyed grace, but I learned a lesson.

4. **Young people are often naïve and potentially rascally.** It's our duty to keep coaching them. If you have teenagers, keep coaching them. They believe they know everything. The fact that they are eighteen and have a driver's license or can vote in elections does not make them mature adults. They still need guidance.

5. **There are some things we love that can lead to trouble.** In my naivety, I was demonstrating over lack of water and enjoying myself. I was totally oblivious of the possible consequences. It's important to know that some things we call fun are trouble, and this may be the time to quit.

Chapter 3

Youth Life Encounters

At different times, when graduating from high school and university, I faced the real world. I went job-hunting, got my first job, rented my first apartment, and bought my first car. At each of these points of my life, I had some amazing encounters and life-changing experiences. They represented training in the school of wisdom, and I call them turning points that welcomed me to the real world. They enriched my life and left sweet smiles ultimately at the end.

Welcome to my turning-point stories, and be ready to laugh.

"Young Man, Do Not Spend Your Money"

I had just graduated from high school. I got a job as an auxiliary teacher in a elementary school in my village. My salary was a minimum wage of about N100 per month, or the equivalent of two hundred dollars at the time.

I looked forward to spending my first paycheck. I planned to invite friends for drinks, and to buy clothes for my mum and myself. I planned to furnish my bedroom in the village with electronics, including radio sets, cassette recorders, and a TV. I had a grand spending plan.

All my plans were aborted the first day I resumed work as a teacher. A senior teacher approached me during my lunch break and asked me to see him after school. I honored the invitation. He sat me down and tutored me on life, using himself as a reference point. He told me he made a blunder in life that he still regretted. He got a job similar to what I had and threw wild parties, furnished his apartment lavishly, and became the toast of the female teachers. One of them became pregnant, and he was compelled to marry her at a young age. What a story!

By now, he had three children, his education was limited, and he could barely train his children in school. He missed an opportunity to attend university, as he was weighed down by the financial burden of parenthood. He told me he was an unfulfilled and depressed man, and he knew his life was the result of his own mistakes.

After narrating his story in tears, he gave me an instruction: "Young man, do not spend your money." He advised me to open a bank account and save all my money. He told me that if I did not furnish my apartment, the ladies would not visit. If they visited once, they would not return. The savings would help me later in life, especially in acquiring a good education.

That advice shaped my destiny. I obeyed his instruction and saved almost all my salary for one year. At that point, I was admitted into university, and my savings funded my tuition and upkeep for the first year and a substantial part of the second year. I was grateful for the timely advice from that teacher.

Life Lessons

1. **There is no alternative to savings.** Handle your ATM cards and online-payment platforms with love and caution. The money you save now will help you in the future.

2. **Delayed gratification leads to availability of future resources.** Save while you are still young, and you will have enough money and time to enjoy it when you get older.

3. **Listen to and learn from elders.** An African proverb says that what an elder sees while sitting down, a young man may not be able to see while standing. Always seek counsel before you make critical decisions, so you may be wise at the end. Every purpose is established by counsel.

Learn from my experience as a primary-school teacher. Save and invest, even if it means delayed enjoyment. The best holiday resorts have not been made. The most beautiful people are not yet born. The best cars have not been built. The smartest phones have not been designed. Today is more beautiful than yesterday, and tomorrow will be more beautiful than today. No matter how smart you are, someone has passed the route you want to navigate before you. Get counsel from them. Learn from their mistakes. You will come out better, happier, and more fulfilled in life.

National Youth Service Experience

I was posted to Benin to serve the nation under the mandatory National Youth Service Corps (NYSC) scheme as a teacher. This presented a few personal challenges, as I had no real teaching experience. It was a remedial/continuing-education school.

The next challenge was accommodation. Where would I live? I had never lived on my own before. How was I going to pay the rent? The most challenging personal issue was eating; I had never cooked in my life. I have five sisters, and they did the cooking along with my mother. I didn't even know how to boil an egg. I worried over these issues but was also excited about making new friends and my newfound personal independence.

I was assigned to teach economics and accounting, and I adjusted to the new challenge. My experience at teaching extramural classes during the long vacations while I was an undergraduate student helped build my confidence a little. Surprisingly, the feedback was that the students loved my teaching style, and many excelled in their external examinations.

The accommodation challenge was miraculously solved, as the institution provided fully furnished living quarters for their youth corps participants. I was delighted. But the feeding challenge was not so settled. Initially, I was living on soft drinks and biscuits, but that wasn't satisfying. Then I started eating in small restaurants, but that made no economic sense, as my salary was exhausted by the middle of the month. I eventually went home to my mother for a quick tutorial on how to cook.

My first attempt at cooking on my own nearly ended in disaster. I followed my mother's instructions until I needed to run to the sitting room to watch a TV program, and then forgot I was cooking. Shortly, the kitchen was filled with smoke. The soup was burnt, and the pot was red hot, with nothing to salvage. It was a disappointing experience. I then decided to befriend another participant who would cook for both of us while I contributed money.

Life was getting better—but one day, we received a quit notice from the school authorities, with one month's notice to leave the corps lodge. We refused to accept this, as it was primary host's responsibility to provide us with accommodation. We wanted an allowance to enable us to rent a house in the city and decided to visit the rector to politely state our demands. I was chosen to be the spokesman.

We were ushered into the meeting, and I began to speak. There were ten of us. By the time I finished laying out our appeal, the rector was angry. He threatened to return us back to the secretariat.

While he was still raging, another of our group members spoke. He disowned the group's ideas and stated that he'd had no idea of what we had come to discuss. He asked to be left out of any punishment the rector may want to hand down to us. But in fact, he was the one who'd initiated and coordinated our meetings. I had never seen betrayal in my life before. It was a day to remember. We walked out of the rector's office with our heads bowed. We had to individually rent houses near the institute. I will never forget that experience. Interestingly, I eventually coped well, even with the greater responsibility and independence of living alone.

Life Lessons

1. **Home habits are great.** I didn't learn to cook at home because my sisters were there to do it. I suffered for that. Meanwhile, the guy who was literally using my money to cook for both of us had fun. He was domesticated, and it paid off for him.

   All children must learn how to do everything at home, including cooking, laundry, and other household chores. You don't know when they will need these abilities. Teach your children home management skills irrespective of their gender.

2. **There is always a betrayer.** We thought we were united until we realized there was a betrayer amongst us. Those who betray a common cause destroy the unity of a group. In life, you will always meet people like that. Make provision for them. Expect there to be one even when you hold family or confidential office meetings. Be circumspect. Trust others, but never trust absolutely. Only God can be trusted absolutely.

3. **Old skills can help the future.** When I was teaching extramural classes, I was ignorant of the fact that I was acquiring skills I would need in the future. It gave me courage to face a large class of far older and more

experienced students and to teach alongside professionally qualified lecturers. Keep learning; keep yourself busy. Learn to drive. Learn another language. Learn tailoring. Learn to build. Learn to paint. Learn to swim. Learn photography. Become technologically savvy. Just keep learning. One day, what will make you stand out and give you an edge over others may be that additional skill you have.

4. **Challenges will always come.** Sometimes the unexpected happens. When it does, we must rise to face it with confidence. I was not prepared for the challenge of leaving the corps lodge. Welcome to the real world. Be prepared with an option B and sometimes an option C. Life is filled with challenges. But you must make up your mind to handle each day as it comes. God's mercies are new every morning. By the grace of God, you will overcome every challenge that life throws at you.

My First Apartment

I got my first rented accommodation after my first job. It was ten minutes' walk from the ever-busy Ikorodu Road. I rented one room in a three-floor apartment complex occupied by different families and individuals. The landlord and his family lived on the topmost floor.

While living in this complex, I had a kerosene stove. There was a common kitchen for all tenants, and one problem we faced was the theft of kerosene. Because I often left early for work and returned late, thieves would steal my kerosene directly from the stove by emptying it into theirs. In some cases, they just used up my kerosene by cooking on *my* stove. I never caught them.

Additionally, we shared a bathroom and a toilet on the first floor. It was there I learned that some people can spend hours in the bathroom. It can be irritating, especially early in the morning when there is a long queue, and everyone wants to catch a bus to get to work. I learned to wake up early to avoid delays.

This house was where I saved for and bought my first bed after sleeping on a mattress for six months. The day I took delivery of the bed was a day of great excitement. I also bought a ceiling fan that went on to serve me for the next twenty years without maintenance.

I had been living in that room for two years when my boss mentioned her plan to buy a new remote-control TV set. She offered to sell me her manually operated TV at a discount to enable her to supplement her purchase. I was thrilled with my new TV.

I qualified as a chartered accountant in that room. I got a good banking job in that room. Finally, I bought my first car, an eight-year-old Honda Accord. I borrowed money from my office and two friends to buy the car. Immediately after I bought it, the landlord gave me a quit notice. He told me that there was no parking space to accommodate my car and I had to move.

Life Lessons

1. **Don't despise your humble beginnings.** I no longer live in a one-room apartment, but that was where I started. In fact, my journey to marriage started there. I started cooking with kerosene stoves before gas cookers. I was once without a bed or a ceiling fan or a television. There was a time when I had no car and relied solely on public transportation.

    But by the grace of God, things have changed. Everyone who is successful was once what appeared to be a failure. Everyone who is big was once small. Start small. Stay at it. One day, by the grace of God, you will become successful.

2. **You will deal with all kinds of people.** In a multitude, you will find the good, the bad, and the ugly. It was the

same at the house I lived in. The diversity of people there included the elderly neighbors who advised me about life, a successful bank auditor who I admired and looked up to, and colleagues who encouraged me as we studied together to become chartered accountants. Then there were the strange ones who stooped so low as to steal kerosene. When you are in a multitude, make provision for all kinds of people. Learn to live with and cope with them. It's normal; just remain focused.

3. **One man's meat is another's poison.** My boss was tired of using a TV without remote control and upgraded to a remote-control TV. Meanwhile, I was eager to own any TV at all, since I didn't have one. What my boss was willing to discard was a treasure to me. What is useless to someone may be just what someone else has been praying for. Never throw away anything. Nothing is useless. Find someone who needs it.

4. **Savings will lead to investments.** I was able to acquire my household furniture through installment payments. That's one way to save. There was no credit facility available. I was depositing money with bed makers and ceiling-fan sellers. It took time. But one day, those items became mine. Anything you want to acquire can be yours if you start saving toward it. The only bridge between you and your dream property is savings and time. If you have both, one day your home will be filled with all you've been dreaming of.

5. **Not everyone is happy with your success.** My landlord appeared to love me until I bought a car. The urgency with which he dispatched a quit notice to me was unprecedented. I'd had no plan to park my car in the premises. There was no place to park cars there anyway.

Do not think everyone will rejoice when you make progress. Life is like that. In fact, you will get a lot of opposition when you begin to make progress. Pastor J. T. Kalejaiye's quotes are very instructive here. He said, "When you are on top, you become the topic," and "In life, you must choose either to be envied or pitied."

In a football game, the player in possession of the ball will be constantly tackled. If people are contending with you, you must be carrying something valuable. That's life. Live with it and do not bear grudges.

Changing House

Many years ago, I traveled to the United States on a US-government-sponsored training. I returned to Lagos immediately afterward. At the baggage area, I was waiting for my suitcases when I introduced myself to a man standing next to me, and we got to talking. I found out he was a senior pastor. I told him I was on official transfer from Port Harcourt to Lagos and was presently searching for a house, as I had to move out of the temporary residence provided by the company I worked for. He told me he'd just bought a house in Lekki, a highbrow neighborhood, and would be moving there soon.

We exchanged cards, and he said, "Who knows, you may be the one to take over my old home." We laughed and said our goodbyes, and I soon forgot all about him.

A few months later, I had a strong impression to locate the man's church, as I was searching for a place of worship in Lagos. I located him, and he was pleased to see me. He offered me his home. He had just moved to his new house, and he even gave me the privilege to determine how much rent I was willing to pay. I gladly accepted and moved in with my family.

One year later, I visited him in his home and fell in love with the location. I told him I desired to live there. In less than a month, he found a house close to his that was available for sale. I took out a mortgage and bought the house. It's been twenty years, and I still live behind the man I met at the airport. We have become not only neighbors but also family friends.

Life Lessons

1. **There are no chance or casual meetings.** Everyone God brings in close contact with you is in your life for a purpose. There is no perfect location, opportunity, weather, or timing for God's plan. Who would believe that the setting for this life-changing meeting would be the airport?

2. **Be nice to everyone you meet in life.** You don't know who God will use to bless you. That day, I reached out to a stranger to respectfully honor and greet him. That greeting opened doors to discussions that progressed to him securing two accommodations for me, one as a tenant and another as an owner. Be nice to people and respect elders. Engage people. Cheer people up when they are down. You can't tell how far those casual discussions can go.

3. **Follow up and nurture relationships.** If I had not gone looking for the man in his church, the airport discussion would not have progressed further. Many times, we strike relationships, but we don't follow up. Use phone calls, personal visits, and social media platforms to oil relationships. Many people have been placed on your path of life to assist you. They may not be able to help you now, but you don't know what they will do in the future. Cultivate relationships.

4. **Learn to speak out when in need.** As soon as I saw the pastor's home, I expressed interest in living in that neighborhood, and he made it happen. Don't fail to speak out if you have a need. The worst answer you will get is

no, and *no* does not diminish you in any way. It only means try again. Meanwhile, it opens up the possibility of a *yes*.

If you ask, you will receive. If you seek, you will find. If you knock on the door, it will be opened to you. Those who don't ask, don't receive. Those who do not seek, do not find. Those who do not knock on the door will be facing closed doors. Be wise.

My First Self-Owned Home

I was offered a beautiful new home in a gated community. The offer price was high, and I couldn't afford it. I was inspired by faith to apply for a mortgage loan from my employer, even though there was an embargo on staff loans at the time. Three days later, there was an official memo from the CEO informing staff that the embargo had been lifted and my loan application was granted. Within a short while, I had paid for my house.

I shared the good news with a friend of mine, and he asked for my help to locate a property for sale within the same estate. I found one for him, he applied for his own mortgage, which was approved, and he too moved in with his family.

It's been twenty years, and I still live in that house. My office friend who bought his own house through my advice remains a close friend. His home is less than one minute's walk away from mine. When God wanted to restore me and lift me up, he was the one who gave me a strong recommendation. Today, I feel highly indebted to him.

Life Lessons

1. **Never stop trying.** I knew there was an embargo on staff loans when I applied for the mortgage loan from my company, but I tried nonetheless. I believe that request led to

the lifting of the embargo. Many times, we give up without trying. I remember my secondary school motto: "Either I find the way, or I make one." That motto still guides me. We were taught never to accept *no* for an answer and that if the door is shut, we should try the windows. If the windows are shut, we can make a door through the walls.

Even if you receive a *no*, try again. When the traffic light indicates red, it doesn't mean you should make a U-turn. It only means you have to wait a little while, and the same traffic light will change to green. Never accept defeat. Keep trying.

2. **Be a blessing to others.** I am grateful that I visited my office friend to ask him to apply for a mortgage. I am glad I shared my joy and became a vessel for giving him his own home. When you receive favor, please extend it to others. Somehow, we reap what we sow. Sixteen years after I assisted him, he gave me a quantum leap in my career by recommending me for a life-transforming job.

Keep doing good works. The harvest will eventually be ready, and the harvest is often far bigger than the seed. You may not always be rewarded by the same person you did good for. God can use anyone to return your harvest. Just keep doing good deeds to others.

My Stockbroker

Many years ago, I decided to buy some shares in the stock market. There was a stockbroker in my estate, and we became friends. I consulted him, and soon enough, I had built a healthy portfolio of stocks.

Years later, when I lost my job and could not secure another one, I authorized my stockbroker to sell all my shares. The firm bought the stocks off me. Part of the unwritten deal was that subsequent dividends on those stocks would belong to the stockbrokers. However, six months after the sale, I erroneously received dividend warrants by post. I immediately paid them into my bank account, received value, and then issued my cheque for the full value in favor of the stockbroking firm, with a cover letter returning the funds.

The CEO of the firm was surprised by my honesty and asked to meet me in person. We met, and he found out I am a pastor. He started attending my church and became an active member. He felt I was the kind of person who should pastor him. We became close friends. One day, a senior pastor's son was having challenges paying his school fees in Europe. I mentioned it to this man, and he paid the fees. Every year, he had a cake delivered on my birthday.

He later relocated to North America but was not done blessing me. One night, he called and offered to sponsor my wife and me on a pilgrimage to Israel. Till today, we remain friends.

Life Lessons

1. **Integrity pays.** When I refunded that money, I didn't have a job. I was literally living from hand to mouth. But I had to keep my word. Whatever it costs you, keep your commitments. It's not an option; it's mandatory. Whether it's convenient or not, keep your word.

2. **Live what you preach.** I am a pastor, and I preach holiness and integrity. I didn't know that would be the basis for a man and his family to join our church. You may not be a preacher like me, but you are a role model. As a parent, do you do what you tell your children not to do? As a team lead in the office, are you an example for your team? People are watching you, and you may not even know. The patronage and loyalty you receive will depend on what you do and not what you say.

A Future Pastor Attends Seminary

I was transferred by my employer to Port Harcourt. I identified a parish of my church to attend. It was called the Redeemed Christian Church of God, the King's Palace, and it was barely two minutes' drive from my office. At the end of my first visit, those of us worshipping there for the first time were taken to an inner welcome room and offered refreshments. The welcome team was very friendly, and I fell in love with the church from that day.

My wife did not immediately join me in my relocation to Port Harcourt, as she was living overseas at the time. I anticipated that my weekends and evenings would be boring without my family. My concern was how to manage the idle time and the potential temptations of being a successful bank manager and not having my family living with me, if you know what I mean.

While I was troubled about this, help came. In church the following Sunday, an announcement was made for admission applications to the church's Bible college. The course would run for one year, and lectures would be held in the evenings and on weekends. It was a perfect program for me.

My purpose for registering for the course was to kill boredom. But after enrolling, I was shocked to see from the contents of the syllabus that it was a seminary or a training program for would-be pastors. I had no calling to be a pastor, and I wondered what I was doing there. I was upset with myself for not doing my due diligence—but then I realized there was no harm in attending. I completed the program but didn't bother to ask for the certificate, because I believed I wouldn't need it.

A year later, I had a vision. I saw myself at a pulpit preaching the gospel to a large crowd. It made no sense to me when I woke up. About a month later, I had another vision. The general overseer of my church, Pastor E. A. Adeboye, was visiting Port Harcourt, and people were lined up to shake hands with him. I was at the rear. All those who shook hands with him just moved on after the handshake. However, when it was my turn, he held me tight, turned to my pastor, and said, "This is the man we have been looking for." My pastor nodded in agreement. I woke up, and again, I couldn't understand the dream.

Barely three months after these night visions, I was leaving church after the service when my pastor stopped me. He told me that God had a need for me. One thing led to another, and I became a worker in the mission. Two years later, I was ordained as a deacon. Fast-forward twenty-four years and, by the grace of God, I became a senior pastor in the mission. Interestingly, before I could be promoted to senior pastor, one of the requirements was for me to produce evidence of having graduated from the Bible college. I had to trace my Bible college principal, and it took nearly a month of searching through piles of papers for my twenty-four-year-old Bible college certificate to be located.

Twenty-two years after I had those visions, I was privileged to preach at the mission headquarters, called the *redemption camp*. I preached to a live crowd of nearly half a million people, with possibly millions of others watching live on cable TV and other platforms. I recollected my visions of preaching to a large crowd. During the message, I told them the story of how it took twenty-two years for my vision to manifest. A vision received from God will eventually come to pass, regardless of any delays.

Life Lessons

1. **Visions are for an appointed time.** Visions, if pursued, will eventually come to pass. It may take time, but don't give up. It may cost resources in energy, finance, and time. Stay at it. You will one day watch a playback of your visions in the physical realm.

2. **Keep busy. Don't waste time.** Find something important to occupy yourself with. No knowledge is ever wasted. I am grateful that I tried to occupy myself with something I considered important some twenty-four years ago. I never imagined it would be useful to me in the future. Please get busy. Time that is wasted is lost forever. If you wisely use your spare time, you will one day in the future be glad you did.

3. **Take one step at a time.** When they received me warmly on my first day in church, no one, including myself, knew they were welcoming someone who would in the future become a senior pastor in the mission. I dismissed my visions as lacking in meaning. However, gradually, one step at a time, the journey started, and here we are. Never despise the days of humble beginnings.

Chronic Fatigue Syndrome

I was an assistant manager in a new-generation bank. I was in my twenties, single, living alone, and working extremely hard. I had a passion to succeed and a hunger to excel, and sometimes I worked into the weekend.

After about six months of this highly stressful job, I fell ill. The sickness was unusual. I lost my appetite and could barely sleep. All kinds of tests were carried out at the hospital, and I was referred to a senior consultant. He asked me to do several more tests, and at the end of the results, he came out with an unusual diagnosis: there was nothing medically wrong with me.

But I was not getting better. The consultant had no option but to refer me to an in-house psychologist. I met with him, and he asked me a couple of apparently mundane questions. As I answered, he kept plotting a graph. From my answers, we both realized that I barely ate well, I never exercised, and my work hours were beyond normal.

At the end of our forty-five-minute chat, the psychologist told me I was suffering from chronic fatigue syndrome. He advised me to start exercising, cut down my workload, and improve my meals. I started playing table tennis, and to my surprise, after the first game, I slept well. So I played every evening. My low appetite and low energy also disappeared. In less than two weeks, I was fully recovered.

Life Lessons

1. **Exercise has no alternative.** Our bodies are configured to be exercised. Work is good but must be balanced with regular exercise. I learned this lesson early. Today, when people see me ride my bicycle or walk, they think it's for fun. Far from it. Make sure you exercise regularly to prevent problems from a sedentary lifestyle.
2. **Some sicknesses do not require medications.** Our natural inclination is to ask for medicines when we are not well. Sometimes a change in lifestyle will do the job.
3. **Watch your workload.** Work smart. I had no weekends then and worked late into the night. Our bodies are not configured to keep working without rest. Resting for at least one whole day in a week is not an option; it is mandatory. Respect closing times. Both our mind and physical body need time to shut down.

Chapter 4

Marriage Stories

Parents rarely take time to teach their children about marriage. Most young couples' marriages are based on observation of their parents'. Few couples read books on marriage, while a few others have the opportunity of counseling. Someone once said that marriage is the only school where you receive your certificate the same day you enroll in the school, and from which you never graduate. Many end up learning in marriage what they should have learned before marriage. This is one reason many married people are enduring marriage instead of enjoying marriage.

I made mistakes in my marriage, and I learned from those mistakes. To date, I've been married happily for thirty years and counting. Here are my marital stories that may encourage and inspire you.

Attempted Marriages

Before I got married, I made some unsuccessful attempts at finding a spouse. I am grateful to God that they failed. One almost succeeded but for God's help. The lady cheated on me three times; I found out and forgave her each time. One day, we went to watch a match, and she left the stadium with another man. When she returned four hours later to beg for forgiveness, I had closed both my physical door and marital door to her. I'm glad that I refused to be appeased on that matter despite strong delegates that were sent to appeal.

The second one was someone who was ready when I was not ready. She was in my house every weekend. She knew where I kept the keys to my apartment. She would come in on Saturdays, sleep, eat, and wait for me, to no avail. I would leave for my chartered accountant professional qualifying examination lectures early each Saturday and return late at night. Many times, I slept over in the classroom studying. I did this for two years.

When she kept coming and I was not available, she disconnected. I remember her last note. She realized I had no time for her, and so she was saying a final goodbye. I respect this wonderful lady for making that decision, because at that time, my focus did not include a social life. I was determined to become a chartered accountant no matter the cost. I achieved my ambition. It was four years after I became a chartered accountant that I finally got married.

Life Lessons

1. **Early warning signs.** In my opinion, the worst thing that can happen to a person in marriage is for the spouse to cheat. While courting, please watch out for the early warning signals. It's impossible for a zebra to cover up its stripes. It's impossible for a snake not to crawl on its belly. Goats must eat grass. No matter the cover up, one day you will see warning signs. Do not ignore them. Investigate them, and you will come up with real evidence.

   Whatever you cannot live with in marriage, please do not tolerate or overlook in courtship. Everything you see in courtship is a sample of the bigger picture that will eventually manifest in marriage. Choose wisely.

2. **It takes two to tango.** If one person is ready for marriage but the other person is not, the marriage cannot work. In my story, the lady was ready, but I wasn't. I was ambitious and needed to settle myself before bringing someone into my life. I wanted to achieve my professional goal first. I knew that marriage and kids would require my attention day and night, and I would be unable to study.

   There is a time for everything. Know yourself. Rearrange your priorities. Even though this lady was a wonderful person, my professional ambition was at the top of my priorities.

3. **Courtship has no alternative.** Courtship is essential for marriage. Never marry without knowing the character of the person you will live with for the rest of your life. That's one of the reasons for courtship. If you notice things you can't live with, take appropriate action.

Hello, Good Girl

I was no more comfortable living alone. I had this strong desire to get married. I was restless and lonely. I was tired of inviting my cousin to cook for me.

Then I visited my uncle's wife, and I shared my burden with her. I asked her for suggestions and told her the only qualifications were that the lady must come from a good family and have a university degree. Nothing else was important to me.

She recommended a lady who had a national certificate of education, but I quickly told her no. Then she mentioned a second option, someone I realized I had met. That second option is my wife today, and we have been happily married for about thirty years.

How did it happen? Eleven years before, I met a man called George (may God bless his soul). We became friends and enrolled in university at the same time. The friendship continued even after graduation. While on campus, I visited him at home. He had a young sister, Ijeoma, who was always reading novels. We barely exchanged greetings. She was still in high school, while we were already graduates. This was the same lady that my uncle's wife recommended to me for marriage.

I didn't know much about her, but I was willing to get more information. I asked my uncle's wife about her education. She didn't know but asked her oldest daughter, who told us that the woman in question was working on being admitted for a master's degree program at the University of Jos. As soon as I heard this, I went to her brother's office and sought permission to visit her. He granted it, and I flew to Jos.

We met, and I was shocked that she remembered me. I left for Lagos the next day. In less than six months, we were married. We have been blessed with four wonderful children and a happy marriage.

Life Lessons

1. **Never burn bridges.** When I met George years ago and we became good friends in university, little did I know he would be my brother-in-law. I'm grateful I met George and for our friendship. If we were not close, he would not have given me a written note to his sister. George is gone to heaven now, but I am eternally grateful to God for our friendship.

   Never destroy a bridge; you don't know when you will need to cross it again. Nurture relationships and keep in contact with old friends. There must be a reason God made you meet someone.

2. **Look for a divine connection.** When God put the burden on me to visit my uncle's wife, He wanted to arrange a divine

connection. That was why my uncle's wife volunteered my wife's name. That was why God made sure that her daughter met my wife-to-be only a few months earlier. God made sure she obtained the critical information that my wife-to-be was completing a master's degree thesis. And the divine connection was done!

Divine connection often works through divine information. You need to know when you're getting critical information and run with it. Additionally, divine connections work through people. When you have a need, do mention it to people you trust. If I had not mentioned my desire to get married to my uncle's wife, she would not have played the role she did. Share your burdens. God is likely to help you through someone close to you.

A problem shared is a problem half-solved. Don't bottle up your problems. God has deposited in someone close to you the right solution to your problems. If you reach out to that person, you will have a testimony.

3. **It takes two to marry.** My wife agreed to marry me after just one meeting. That sounds ridiculous. Why did she accept my proposal? What I did not tell you is that my wife had fasted for forty days praying for a husband. I arrived in Jos on the last day of the fast, completely oblivious of her spiritual exercise. She told me after we got married that she had a vision the night before I arrived. God spoke to her in a dream that her husband would literally walk in looking for her. Less than twelve hours after her dream, I arrived from Lagos knocking at her door.

When I knocked, she opened the door and hugged me. She called me by the nickname given to me by her brother. When I made the proposal, she was not surprised.

Today, when young people want to get married, I ask them to pray separately. It takes the conviction of both to

Chapter 5

Parenting Stories

Being a first-time parent is challenging. I recall the birth of our first baby. It took me time to understand what it takes to be a daddy. The birth of a child is only the beginning of a long journey. Until they become adults, you need to make decisions for them. As they get older, your parenting style will change. You will discuss more with them. You will engage more. But you will still pick up their bills.

I learned a lot watching my parents look after me. I have also had my own experiences as a parent. Here are some of my stories on parenting.

"My Son, Never Forget Whose Son You Are"

I was thirteen, and my father had just taken me to high school. It was my first time leaving home, and I was apprehensive. I was not sure what the future would hold, what kind of friends I would make, or how I would cope far away from home.

My dad ensured I was settled in my dormitory, and just before he left, he drew me close. He asked me by what means of transportation we came to the school. That was obvious, and I told him it was by public transport. He asked me to look around and note how a few other students came in exotic cars, some of them chauffeur-driven. I nodded. Then my dad said, "Whatever you do in this school, never forget whose son you are." Immediately after he made this profound statement, he waved and left for the bus stop to return to his base.

That statement hit me like a bomb and became my guiding philosophy in life. In university, when I was tempted to make a wrong decision or cross a forbidden line, those words became a restraining force reverberating in my head. I became friends with many students from rich backgrounds in the university and watched as some were carried away by their newfound freedom to do wrong.

My father's statement meant a lot to me. He was a man of few words, but on the few occasions he spoke, his words were weighty. I still remember his words today, and I was twenty-seven when he died. My father was only reminding me not to forget my family background.

The poor must never forget their roots no matter where they find themselves. Even the rich and privileged must not forget their roots. Otherwise, the family empire can collapse in their hands.

Life Lessons

1. **Never forget your parents' advice.** Nobody can give you better advice than your parents. Believe me, your parents love you, and they want you to succeed. No matter how old you are today, you are still a son or daughter of your parents. You should not only listen to them, you should obey them.

2. **Parents, spend quality time with your children.** During the holiday season, please hold private sessions with your children. Fathers are particularly guilty of not speaking enough with their children. I call on all guilty fathers to repent today and speak words of correction,

encouragement, and counseling to their children. Most gifts we buy them will not last more than a couple of years. But words of wisdom we sow into their lives will last a lifetime.

Fathers, use this period to ask for the examination result sheets of your children. Look out for their teachers' comments, especially on their conduct. My dad has gone to heaven, but his words still guide me today.

More than forty-seven years later, no matter the level of success God has gracefully enabled me to attain, for which I am eternally grateful, I still remember whose son I am. Please remember whose you are. This will help you to be humble and raise your children better.

The world is hurting. We must do our best to heal it. We must bring back hope, peace, and joy. God gave us a beautiful planet. We must use it well and make everyone happy. If all parents teach their children, the world will have greater harmony and peace.

I Trust You, My Son

I was sixteen and in the fourth year of my five-year high school. I consistently failed mathematics. My average score each academic term was 18 percent. The sordid performance in mathematics weighed adversely on my overall performance.

I'll tell you why I consistently failed mathematics: it was nothing but bad company. I started hanging out with a group of rascally boys who were a little older and who I looked up to. They told me that mathematics was the toughest subject in the world and there was no point in studying it, so we didn't study, and we all consistently failed together.

In my fourth year, our rascality graduated to defiance. These guys suggested that we should stay away from the math class altogether. Their argument, which made sense to me then, was that we should use that time to take a siesta and get refreshed for the next subject, which we could easily pass.

So just before the math class, we would jump through a window and go to the hostel to take a nap. We didn't know some eagle-eyed teachers took note.

Our parents were summoned by the principal, who narrated our bad behavior to them. My father was made to sign an understanding that the school was at liberty to expel me if I ever missed the math class or jumped through a window again.

I expected problems when my father left the principal's office. Rather, I was shocked when my father said he did not believe the principal. Really? He said he knew his son and that he trusted me and would always trust me. He told me he believed in me. I was perplexed as I watched him leave.

That day, I resolved not to disappoint him again. How could I disappoint my dad if he trusted me that much? I went back to math class. I began to listen attentively for the first time in three years. To my surprise, I started grasping a few things. My performance improved significantly.

You may not believe it, but mathematics became my best subject in the final year in the same school. I made an A1 in my GCE exams, and I began to coach others in math. Eventually, I went on to study finance in university and became a chartered accountant a few years after graduation.

Life Lessons

1. **Watch out who your children's friends are.** I made friends with the wrong boys in boarding school. They had bad behaviors, and they encouraged me to join them. I'm grateful for the push to break up my relationship with them. School friends will always have a massive influence

on each other. If parents observe a major adverse pattern with their children, they need to check the type of friends those children have.

2. **Positive reinforcements from parents help.** Even when parents are disappointed, they should still boost the self-esteem of their children. Affirmations elevate self-confidence. My father's statement that he trusted me was a turning point in my life.

3. **Our Father in heaven never gives up on us.** My father's role in this story reminds me of the role of God the Father in our lives. Do you know that even if you are living in sin now, God still loves you? He is only waiting for you to repent and reconcile with Him. Do yourself a favor and don't give up on yourself. You will make it despite the mistakes you've made in the past. Your children will make it. Keep believing in them like my father believed in me thirty-eight years ago. If I could excel in math, there is nothing you cannot achieve.

My Daughter and University Education

My second daughter was admitted to a top university. We rejoiced but then wept at the same time, because I did not have a regular paying job and couldn't afford the fees. I had a consulting job, but the income was highly irregular and unpredictable.

The first hurdle was to pay a five-hundred-dollar acceptance fee, which we did not have. I called up a relative who promised to help. The money came in, but it was less than the amount promised. It was also in local currency, meaning I had to convert it to US dollars and add a transfer fee. We couldn't do all this in the two days left to make the payment. I was in a fix.

Then I remembered a cousin of mine, Lorreta. I made an SOS call to borrow five hundred dollars and asked her to transfer it to the college office. I explained my dire situation. It was a Friday, and the acceptance fee had to be received on or before Monday. She told me two things were in my favor: one, she had just received her paycheck, and two, her bank was open for a few hours on Saturday. Gladly, she was able to help, and the first hurdle was crossed.

The first installment of the tuition was the next hurdle: it was due in three weeks. I showed the bill to my boss and lifetime friend, Aunty Mo. She not only encouraged me but took care of that deposit. It was an amazing miracle, and it was not a loan—it was a gift. We danced and rejoiced at home.

A bigger installment of the tuition was due in a month. There was nowhere else to turn for help, so we had to look up to heaven. Suddenly, my wife had an idea. She asked me to take the title documents of our house to an old client of mine and offer to sell our house to his company so they could use it as their guesthouse. We would then use the proceeds to train our children in school. The man had been my client for over fifteen years, and I always supported him because he was extremely hardworking.

I made him the offer, and his response shocked me. He was upset that I hadn't let him know earlier that I had financial challenges. He stated that he admired my integrity, as I had never asked him for a favor for as long as we had been friends. He refused to buy the house but rather paid my daughter's tuition for the full year. He also promised to pay for the following year if I didn't have a job by then.

By the special grace of God, three months after this amazing divine favor, I got a full-time job. When I look back and reflect on these miracles, I can only give God thanks.

Life Lessons

1. **Believe in miracles.** When you hit a dead end, you can only hope for a miracle. For me, help came from unexpected quarters. That's a miracle. Where I sought a loan or tried

to sell my house, I rather got a gift. That's a miracle. How else can you describe a miracle? If you have nowhere else to go, look up to heaven. Miracles still happen.

2. **God is never late.** We thought we were late; we were on the edge, but help came at the eleventh hour.

3. **Never give up.** When there was no other option but to sell my house, I dusted the documents off and went straight to a potential buyer. I just felt giving up was not an option. Whatever you are passing through now, please hold on. Never consider quitting. Keep thinking of options. Hold on. You will make it if you don't quit.

4. **Integrity pays.** Integrity is like a savings account: one day you will draw from it when you most need it. I had dealt with this client with utmost professionalism. I didn't know he was watching and that God would answer my prayers through him. I encourage you to continue to be honest and professional. Maintain your integrity at the highest level. Yours may not happen exactly the way mine did, but you will laugh last.

Onitsha Trader Apprentice

Years ago, I graduated from senior high school. My father was a poor trader and felt he had given me his best with regard to education. As soon as I completed high school, my father invited me to join him in his shop. His plan was for me to be a part of his business, first as an apprentice and then, later, taking over. I learned quickly, and the business began to grow. My father was delighted.

After a few months, however, I lost interest in the business. My heart kept telling me that I was in the wrong place and doing the wrong thing. I dared not tell my father how I felt, but I was unhappy and dissatisfied.

I devised a strategy to get out of the shop. Instead of soliciting for customers, I read newspapers and ignored customers when they passed by. I started going to the shop late. Within one week, my loss of interest in the business was evident to my father, and he told me to stay away.

In the interim, I received news of my friends enrolling in university. I felt low. Then an opportunity became available. I heard about a government program where recent high school graduates were being hired as auxiliary teachers to bridge the massive shortage of teachers in elementary and high schools. Short-term training was available to ramp up the skills of the graduates.

I applied, and with the assistance of a distant relative, I was hired and posted to work in an elementary school in my village. It was some distance from home and was the same school I had attended as a younger child. The same headmaster was still there. My journey to destiny started in that school. I worked there for one year and saved all my salary, which I used to support my entry into university.

Life Lessons

1. **Always listen to your inner conviction.** When my heart told me I had no future in trading, I had to act fast. If I hadn't made that decision, I would not be writing this book today. God does not shout. When you lack peace of mind in what you are doing, it's time to move. Delay can cause you irreparable damage.

2. **You can communicate your message politely.** Some children could have been confrontational and lacking in respect when passing their preferences to their parents. I communicated my message with wisdom and diplomacy. I was only eighteen, but I knew what would upset my father and avoided it. I always tell young people to study their

parents and avoid making them unhappy. Learn to walk with wisdom.

3. **Make good friends and relate with them.** My friends were a good source of information for the job I secured as a teacher. Your schoolmates can be a powerful resource base. Do not disconnect from them. If you can, attend alumni meetings. Maintain your social network. Everything you need in life lies with someone. The information to link you with that person is often with someone else. Relate with people.

A Rough Ride

My first son was a special breed—smart and full of humor. I named him *Chukwuemeka*, which means "God has done a great job." Indeed, he lived up to his name. He started nursery school quite ahead of his peers. I recall waking him up daily at age four, at five o'clock in the morning, to enable him to ride with me to school on my way to work. His school was close to my office. He was already a shining star in preschool.

However, when he was six years old, tragedy struck. He lost his appetite and started losing weight rapidly. Gradually, we noticed his tummy was protruding. We knew something was wrong. We took him to the hospital and received shocking news: he had a form of cancer called *neuroblastoma*. Unbelievable.

We were encouraged to take him to another hospital. After nearly three years of chemotherapy, he was cleared and discharged. We were told he needed a yearly checkup for the next five years. Exactly one year later, when we returned for a checkup, we received more tragic news: the cancer was back, and it was terminal. A few months later, he was dead.

Pain followed along with grief and the agony of sleepless nights. My late father was the only close blood relative I had lost. Now the loss was my only son. It hurt deep in my marrow. It was much more painful because we'd had the good news that he was free of cancer. Somewhere within me, the pain still lingers till today.

Exactly six years later, my wife conceived, and we had another boy. Those who knew the boy could tell that this was a replica of the first boy. This was a heavenly gift to wipe away the tears of the past, and we give glory to God.

Life Lessons

1. **Tough times help others.** Being a parent can be tough. The loss of my son hurt deeply. Maybe the worst experience a parent can ever have is to plan the funeral of a child. That loss, however, helps me in encouraging people today who may face a similar challenge.

2. **There is still hope.** It is not over until it is over. Six years after the loss of my first son, another boy was born. If you are hurting over any issue, please do not give up hope. Even in that dark cloud, there is still some light. We are not in control of issues in our lives. But when we keep hope alive, things have a way of turning around for the good. Restoration is still possible. Bad news can still be turned into good news. That's my desire for you.

Choosing My Children's School

I had just been transferred by my employer to Lagos, a bustling city of 20 million people with a good number of high-end private schools. Immediately after I arrived, I sought counsel from friends and shortlisted two top private elementary schools to be considered. The schools were for the children of upper-middle-class parents.

The next day, I set out to visit one of the schools. I was stopped at the gate and told I could only see the head of the school if I had an appointment. I didn't, but I was determined. They refused to let me drive in despite my appeals, and soon I had to leave.

I headed for the next school and received the same treatment. Then I returned to my friend who had given me the information on the schools. I told him of my experience, and he asked me what kind of car I drove there. I told him, and he laughed. He reminded me that these were upper-class schools. He advised I should visit the same schools with a Mercedes-Benz or any other luxury car, and that would make a difference. I was put off, especially since the fees were already mind-boggling. But the pressure to identify with the upper class was still a driving force.

I went home disappointed and frustrated. But then, by divine inspiration, I remembered an international school owned by a Christian mission, the Redeemer's International School. The fees fit in my budget, the teachers were friendly, the head of school was accessible, and the curriculum was good. Most importantly, they taught the children sound morals alongside academic studies. I had peace of mind.

Before my children graduated from elementary school, the founders of this school had set up a secondary school. My children naturally moved from the elementary school to the high school. Today, the same mission now owns a university.

It was while my children were in high school that I lost my job. I was financially strapped and had to visit this school to negotiate flexible payment terms for the tuition. The school was extremely supportive.

Life Lessons

1. **Cut your coat according to the size of your cloth.** The old proverb means to live within your means. Don't try to live like the Joneses. I nearly made a blunder by trying to force my way into a class where I did not belong. My singular

decision to backtrack from those upper-class schools saved me potential embarrassment when I had no job. Information reaching me much later indicated that those schools would not have offered the flexibility in payment for my children's fees. Live within your means. It will save you headaches in challenging times.

2. **Technical knowledge is not enough.** The upper-class schools offered top-level education. Skills are great, but they are not sufficient for molding a child. Strong moral education and the fear of God combined with strong technical skills will produce the ideal child.

3. **Who is your advisor?** My advisor in choosing my children's school had different values than mine. Telling me to borrow a luxury car for my children to be accepted in a school was clearly wrong. If I had listened to him, I would have been in a financial mess. When I was financially challenged, that school would have asked me to withdraw my child. That would have been highly embarrassing and potentially depressing.

I am grateful that I ignored his counsel. I am grateful I waited to be divinely inspired and made a decision that gave me peace of mind. When you lack peace about a decision, do not make it. Lack of peace is indicative of a problem that could arise in the future.

Chapter 6

Career and Workplace Stories

We spend most of our adult life working either for others or for ourselves. A person with experience of long service is likely to have worked for a minimum of thirty-five to forty years. Naturally, such a man will have many stories shaped within the workplace.

Here are some of my career stories. Many are filled with fun, but the lessons are loaded. They surely will help you in your workplace.

The Postman at Work

My first job as a new graduate was in the courier business. It was not my ideal job, but it was the job that was available. My uncle was a branch manager of a bank, and one of his customers introduced me to the owner of the courier company. That's how I got the job.

I was hired as the assistant manager in charge of accounts and administration. I had a team of a few account clerks who knew the job better than I did, having been there for years. I humbled myself to learn quickly. I learned about the business, it was fun, and I met good people. We ran a unique model, with franchises across the country. They picked and delivered mail on our behalf on a commission basis. Some of them were assigned our branded cars.

One of my earliest assignments was to recover a vehicle from one of the franchisees whose franchise had been terminated due to improper practices. I was only twenty-four at the time and was given the challenging assignment of traveling from Lagos across seven states to recover the Volkswagen Beetle. Planning was detailed. Appropriate legal instruments were perfected in Lagos to be executed in another state.

My driver and I took off in a luxurious bus armed with the documents. It was an eleven-hour journey. The next morning, we met with the previously briefed legal officers and, armed with legal support, hired a bus with security personnel to execute the assignment. The location was three hours from the state capital. When we arrived, we identified ourselves, stated our purpose, and presented the papers from our head office with appropriate identification to recover the vehicle.

We asked for our vehicle, they pointed to it outside, and we took possession of it. By the next day, we were back in Lagos with the company's car. Our security backup had little to do. It looked like a commando operation. We were celebrated and given cash rewards for a job well done. For many months thereafter, that Volkswagen beetle was used to take me around for business, and I really felt good in it.

Life Lessons

1. **Big things start small.** When I graduated from university, I wanted to work in a bank, but the available job was in a courier company. I grabbed the job with both hands. It put food on the table, and the exposure was good. When you desire anything big, you may not get it at the first attempt. Start with what you have. Keep improving yourself and do the job well, but keep looking out for opportunities. One day, you will realize your life ambition.

2. **Young people have a lot of capacity.** When I sit back and reflect on the assignment to recover the vehicle, I marvel at the depth of the risk I took at that age. I wasn't focused on the risk then but was bold and angry about why someone would hold on to our vehicle when we had terminated their contract. I needed justice for my company, and I went for it. Young people, if properly guided by those more experienced, can offer a lot. Young people have energy, are open to new ideas, and are willing to take risks.

3. **Stoop to conquer.** When I took the job as head of accounts, I only had an academic knowledge of accounting. Meanwhile, the staff I was to supervise had several years of experience but no formal education. I humbled myself, learned a lot, and earned their respect. I taught them better and more efficient ways of doing the same thing they had been doing for years.

   When you find yourself in a new environment, humble yourself to understand and understudy. No two places are the same. You can easily run into trouble if you assert your authority too early in the day, without understanding the local issues and the unique ways the new place operates.

Chief Accountant

I worked in the courier company as an accountant. It was an elevated and prestigious position with access to a Volkswagen Beetle car and a driver. My performance appraisal was consistently excellent, and I was soon transferred to an associate company and promoted to chief accountant. I was given access to a minibus, my salary was increased to N720 (about $1,400) a month, and I had more staff to supervise. For a single young man in his early twenties, that was a good position to be in. I rented an apartment and furnished it nicely. Life was good.

However, a few things were fundamentally wrong. Even though I was called a chief accountant, I knew I was deluding myself. I was not yet a chartered accountant. Why did I have that position when I had barely had two years' post-graduate experience? There was a daily conflict within me even though I enjoyed the big pay and perks.

Then I met a good old friend who gave me some valuable information. An American bank was hiring, and I was qualified to apply. I was excited, especially with the promise of training. I applied for the job immediately and was selected.

Then the shockers rolled in. The job was a contract employment and was subject to semiannual review, during which the employer could fire me without notice. To make matters worse, my pay (which was not guaranteed beyond six months) would be 25 percent lower than my current salary. Mathematically, it did not make sense. It defied all logic to accept that job.

However, against all common sense, I did accept it. It marked the beginning of my journey into banking. Instead of being fired after six months, my appointment was confirmed as a permanent full employee. By the mercies of God, I went on to have the privilege of sitting on the boards of three banks as an executive.

Life Lessons

1. **Information is power.** If my friend had not informed me about the unadvertised employment scheme in that bank, I would never have taken advantage of it. We need to cultivate useful friendships. Your worth is in your mailing list. Remain in contact with your friends and value them. Appreciate them. Many of your friends have access to information that can shape your life.
2. **Sacrifice is the key to harvest.** You must deny yourself something to get something bigger. If I did not sacrifice

the job I had, I might never have gotten the one that helped me realize my potential and move toward my destiny. Sometimes, we get carried away with the perks of the present and forget that the harvest of today is the product of the seed that was sown yesterday. If, therefore, we sow today, we will reap a greater harvest tomorrow.

Ask farmers: they know that the harvest must never be fully consumed. Inside your harvest of today is the seed for tomorrow's harvest.

3. **It's necessary to face the truth.** No matter the compliments or flattery we receive, the truth is that we know ourselves better than anyone else knows us. My employers at the courier company called me chief accountant, but I knew I wasn't. I needed more experience. I needed more time to develop myself. So I humbled myself and moved on to another job that would help me grow my career. I refused to deceive myself.

4. **There is a time to take risks in life.** When you are young with fewer bills to pay and less responsibility, that's the best time to take risks. I took those risks because I was young and single. If I failed, I could have tried other options. Young people should be encouraged to take calculated risks. As long as the options are legal and moral, please go ahead and try them out. Without risk, there will be no reward.

Job Relocation

Several years ago, my employer, a medium-sized merchant bank, transferred me out of Lagos to a branch in Port Harcourt. I was already an assistant general manager and felt I had outgrown branch business. Branches were run by deputy managers, and I was shocked to be deployed as a branch manager to start a new branch. Our bank did not have a branch in Port Harcourt, so my job was to start one from scratch, including finding office space and our first customers.

I arrived home that evening with the news that I had forty-eight hours to decide. My wife and I were not happy with what was clearly a demotion from divisional head in the head office to branch manager. Secondly, Port Harcourt was a largely underdeveloped town in those days compared to Lagos. We were particularly concerned about finding good schools for our children in the new location.

I sought counsel from friends and associates. The majority of my advisers told me to resign. Getting another banking job would have been as easy as a phone call at that time. They sensed a witch hunt and believed I was being set up to fail. I could not see any good in my future if I took that transfer.

After deliberating with my wife, and contrary to my friends' opinions, I humbled myself and decided to go. This was in the days of the old ADC airlines. By divine mercy, I narrowly missed the plane that crashed en route from Port Harcourt to Lagos. I arrived in Port Harcourt that morning to search for office space and narrowly missed the flight that crashed. This should have been another compelling reason to call it quits. But I held on.

Eventually, one of the best things that ever happened in my life came about on that transfer. First, the branch prospered so much that we began to host the board of directors meetings in Port Harcourt. The branch became more profitable than all the other branches of the bank put together. The managing director visited the branch at least once a month and confessed that as far as he was concerned, the real head office was now in Port Harcourt. I was celebrated by the bank on a consistent basis. I was initially meant to work there for one year, but the managing director kept me there for five years. From that location, I was not only promoted but was made to oversee all the other branches of the bank.

Additionally, as a person, my life took a dramatic turnaround in that town. I became a minister of God. I won a United States government scholarship for an outstanding African banker. That took me to America for six weeks on attachment and training with the best banks in New York and Philadelphia. My bank sponsored me to Stanford University on an advanced management program. Some of my best friends till today are people I met in Port Harcourt.

Life Lessons

1. **Don't resist transfers or appointments by constituted authorities.** At your job, school, or in church, accept your postings with humility. Do not change them. If you buy a piece of land and they allocate a different one to you, do not argue. Even if the transfers are done out of mischief, accept them. They will turn out for your good if you humble yourself, respect your bosses, and honor God.

2. **Seek counsel from your partner.** Ask family members for advice when you are making critical decisions. Your life partner is likely your best advisor. You have a joint destiny. Do not let others play on your ego and cause you to stumble out of pride.

3. **When you make up your mind, don't be discouraged.** Don't let extraneous events cause you to backslide. The plane crash was enough to discourage me, but I refused to let it. Having put your hand on the plough, never look back, no matter the external noise. Those who look back through the rear mirror while driving may crash. Refuse to be distracted.

The Director and the Rat

While I was working as branch manager in Port Harcourt, the branch became the most successful one in the company. At some point, the company decided to hire a new executive to supervise the branches. Naturally, he developed an interest in the most profitable branch under his supervision and gave indications of his plans to change the leadership of the branch and bring in his friend from outside the company to run it.

This was at the same time as my late son fell sick and was receiving intense treatment. I decided to apply for a vacation so I could take care of him. By this time, I had achieved 200 percent results on my key performance indicators. This executive approved my vacation but went on to recommend confidentially that my appointment be terminated, his reason being that I had been losing concentration in the office since my son fell sick. Thankfully, his recommendation was declined by the CEO.

Then he decided on another plan. He visited my branch for an audit. We had run that branch office for four years transparently and passed all audit checks and balances. When he arrived, we made him comfortable and were ready to start work with him the following morning.

I was awakened with an early-morning distress call from him in which he expressed an urgent need to buy a pair of shoes. New shoes? In this remote part of the country? The best shoes were available in the commercial capital where he was visiting from!

He explained that overnight, some strange rats had eaten his shoes. I felt bad for him. We combed the town and eventually found a pair. They fit perfectly, but to our shock, he jettisoned his audit plans and flew back to Lagos. In less than three months, he resigned his job, and I was promoted to take over from him. The whole sequence of events is still a mystery to me.

Life Lessons

1. **Success elicits envy and enemies.** Success will bring you attention. If you don't want to be envied, do not work to

be successful. If you don't want attention, do not work for success. My branch attracted attention from the executive because it was the most successful branch.

2. **Always keep your records in good shape.** In your journey to success, be transparent. I assure you that your books will always attract unusual scrutiny when you are successful. The audits and checks on my books came about because of my success.

3. **Don't let personal challenges negatively affect your job.** Although my son was terminally ill, I was still focused on my job and delivered on my targets.

4. **Don't expect everyone to be nice to you.** How else can you explain someone trying to get you fired when you have a major family health crisis?

5. **"There is no art to find the mind's construction on the face."** This quote was aptly written by William Shakespeare. The executive sympathized with me over the health challenges of my late son. However, at the same time, he was working behind the scenes to ensure that my pain was multiplied by losing my job, even though I had done nothing to him.

6. **Personal interest should not override corporate interests.** When that happens, the organization's sustainability can be called into question. The executive was consumed with the thought of bringing in his friend to run the office. Nothing else mattered. It's a good thing he left early. He would have hurt the corporation if he had stayed longer.

7. **When you have nobody to fight for you, put your trust in God.** I asked God to help me when I noticed the pressure from the executive. Little did I know that God can use rats too. I pray that God will also rise to help you.

Changing Jobs

I had a dream job with the company I worked with at that time. During the ten years I had worked there, I had received a mortgage loan to buy my home, and I was sponsored for expensive training in top organizations all over the world. I was regularly promoted and assigned key responsibilities. I was fulfilled and planned to stay there until retirement.

Then a few unexpected things happened. The dominant shareholder sold his shares, and with the new owners came a change in corporate culture and significant management squabbles.

One day, I had a dream in which the new owner fired the entire top management team, including myself. I woke up pondering on the dream. That same day, I got a call from an old friend offering me a job in a company he was setting up. I saw that phone call as a confirmation of the dream.

I resigned and accepted the new offer. The old company organized a befitting send-forth party for me. Many members of staff were sad to see me go, and I remember some even wept.

However, less than three months later, the new owner did indeed fire the entire top management staff, exactly as I saw it in the dream. Some wondered if I had gotten a hint of it. Yes, I did, but not from any man on earth.

I started my job in the new place. I worked there for about a year with no salary because the company was unable to obtain the required operating license and never opened for business. I finally left when another job opportunity came calling.

Life Lessons

1. **The ownership of a company is critical to its direction.** The moment that organization changed ownership, everything changed. Before you change jobs, find out who

the real majority shareholders are. The character of the owners will reflect on the management. The new owners were known to be unstable and highly temperamental. It was not long before that started manifesting on the culture of the organization.

2. **If the ownership of your corporation changes, it is time to quickly reappraise your continued stay in the company, especially if you are among the top management staff.** It is quite common for new owners to bring in their own management. The usual slogan is for the new owners to reassure the staff that nobody has anything to worry about as long as they do their job well. That's often a strategy to get as much information as possible from the existing management before letting them go.

3. **You may need to consider quitting the stage when the ovation is loudest.** When I left, I was delivering far beyond my key performance indicators. I was, unofficially, the pastor of the organization. I organized prayers for staff and the organization when they had challenges. Notwithstanding, it was the best time to leave.

4. **The race of life is an individual race.** Make your personal decisions rather than flowing with the crowd. When God spoke to me and I got a confirmation through the phone call, I did not consult anyone. If the One who rules in the affairs of man has spoken to you, there is no need to seek counsel from man.

5. **Procrastination can be expensive.** The dream I had carried a sense of urgency. If I delayed in making a decision, the consequences might have been severe. When you are sure God has spoken to you, please do not delay. Act immediately.

Special Promotion

I needed to change my job. I was a deputy general manager where I worked, but I was divinely led to a medium-sized company. The interview for the new job was grueling, lasted hours, and was with the whole board of directors. By the time they were satisfied with my technical competence, one of them asked a unique question: "So who do we ask about you?"

I gave the names of two prominent references, whom they contacted. I was told that one of them said, "If Simon works with you, then you are blessed." When a multibillionaire gives you this kind of reference, it is settled. I had worked for that billionaire ten years earlier.

I was hired. I had hoped I would be hired at a level above my grade, but I was hired at the same level and accepted the job nonetheless.

One year later, regulators visited the company for the yearly examination. One of their observations was that the company lacked executive capacity. The company had a CEO but no executive directors. The board met and decided to make some changes to comply with the regulator's recommendations and advertised for the position in national newspapers. Many people applied, shortlisting was done, and the board members interviewed the shortlisted candidates.

In the end, they came up with one verdict: "Our employees are far better than the candidates interviewed." This created an opportunity for me, and miraculously, I was elevated from deputy general manager to an executive director.

Life Lessons

1. **Technical competence is not enough.** Your character and social contacts are as important as your technical skills.

The endorsement I received from a prominent man was instrumental to me being hired and subsequently elevated to the board. When I worked for the billionaire for nearly ten years, I did not know I would require his endorsement in the future. Please be careful where you find yourself today. You are writing your résumé daily wherever you work.

2. **You may need to sacrifice today's ambition for tomorrow's reward.** If I had insisted that I must be hired as a general manager, I might have missed that job. Meanwhile, just one year later, I had a double promotion, skipping the same grade I had desperately desired.

3. **Build your technical capacity before you aspire to senior management positions.** Technical and leadership skills are vital for senior positions, as you will be required to lead people daily in proffering solutions. If I had been technically deficient at that grueling three-hour interview, the job-placement process would not have progressed further. Equip yourself. Get knowledge. Build capacity. What you know will drive your success.

New City, New Job

I moved from my village to Lagos after graduation. Most large corporations are in Lagos, so it wasn't unusual for young people in search of top corporate jobs to migrate there. Within two years, I had secured my third job at the subsidiary of an international merchant bank. It was a great organization to work for.

Then I was transferred to Port Harcourt to set up a branch office. Less than a week after I arrived, I met an expatriate who had previously lived in Lagos and who gave me some useful advice. He explained that this was a much smaller town than Lagos, and almost everyone knew each other. Most of the men interacted at the same social clubs, while most of the ladies shopped at the same supermarkets. On Sundays, most people attended either of the key churches.

The upper and middle classes were in regular social contact with each other. He warned that because of this close interaction, gossip literally grew wings and flew into several homes before the end of day. This advice was timely and saved me from potential embarrassment.

Soon after, I met an extremely successful middle-aged man. I established a banking relationship with him, and his business contributed to the growth of the branch exponentially. He believed so much in me and supported my marketing efforts.

I will never forget the day he joined me in my small car and went from office to office, encouraging his friends and associates to establish a business relationship with our bank. They all complied. He was also an advisor and helped to identify and sieve out potentially bad customers.

What he did for me was unbelievable. Today, business schools call this *reference marketing*. At one point in time, the branch was making more profits than all the other branches plus the head office put together.

Life Lessons

1. **No two cities are the same.** Be careful when you relocate to a new city, because you will need to understand its social, economic, and spiritual atmosphere. Be sensitive to those issues. Take time to understand and understudy each new terrain before you start interacting. If I did not meet that man who counseled me early upon my arrival, I might have made grievous errors.

2. **Network marketing is great.** You need endorsers and people with local influence to help you start a business

in a new environment. Every location has its own local champions, so make an effort to get them on your side and help you reach out to others. Our success in Port Harcourt was largely attributable to generous endorsements from the key local champions.

Project Review Trip

Over thirty years ago, our bank gave out a working capital loan for the rehabilitation of a moribund corporation. We were based in Lagos, while the firm was based in the hinterland, many kilometers away, where we did not have a branch. The key promoter of the business was a prominent man in his late sixties. He provided high-valued properties to serve as collateral for the loan, and everything looked OK.

I was a young officer in my twenties and was responsible for managing the relationship. A few months after we disbursed the loan, I decided to take a surprise project-monitoring visit.

On arrival, I found the factory looking like a ghost town. I immediately went to the man's residence, which was empty except for a young lady who introduced herself as his daughter. I engaged her, and she explained that her father had some financial issues overseas and had diverted funds to solve those problems. She confessed that the repayment of our loan was doubtful.

On further enquiry, she informed me that her father was presently receiving a community award that was being partly funded with the proceeds of the loan. She was, obviously, unhappy with her dad, or she wouldn't have shared all that information. I thanked her and left immediately.

I returned to the office and filed a report. We then proceeded to perfect our legal documents over the properties securing the loan. However, when our lawyer arrived in the city to perfect the documents, he was arrested. What we did not know was that as soon as the promoter received the funds, he reported to the police that robbers had visited his home and all his title documents were stolen. And so when our lawyer arrived with the title documents, the police arrested him. We had to hire another lawyer to discharge our lawyer. While this was going on, the promoter fell sick and died.

A new court case ensued with the late promoters' children. We finally proved our case. The family repaid the loan, and the title documents were returned.

Life Lessons

1. **Weak link in a chain.** A chain is only as strong as its weakest link. The weakest link in that family was the disgruntled daughter of the key promoter. She helped us move quickly to recover our loan. I exploited this weak link to my advantage. In your team, be sure you have no weak link. It is, however, impossible to do bad without having a weak link. Do good so that you will not be exposed.

2. **Don't work alone.** One of the greatest risks I made on that trip was to go alone. So many things could have gone wrong if the key promoter was in the house when I arrived. Never engage in this kind of trip alone. Two are always better than one.

3. **A strong reference is not enough.** The key promoter was strongly recommended, but he lacked the most important requirement for credit extension: character. Don't do business with anyone who lacks character. Character has no substitute.

Reverse Sack

In the early nineties, the company I worked for documented my key performance indicators as a part of my contract. It was a highly performance-driven organization, and the industry was also intense due to several aggressive new entrants. Despite this, I still met and exceeded my KPIs.

However, the company's performance was well below its competitors, and its market share was declining month on month. The shareholders gave the CEO a six-month ultimatum to turn the company around. He in turn decided to place some of the key top management staff on technical suspension and gave them six months' notice to meet their targets or be fired.

To my surprise, I was on the list, and given my performance, I smelt some mischief. I did everything possible to meet my revised targets while also quietly searching for another job.

There was no internet in those days, and information was disseminated via the staff notice board on each floor. At the end of the six months' notice, I arrived for work on a Monday morning to a bevy of congratulations from the staff. I wondered why, and they directed me to the notice board. I had just been promoted! Promoted on the day I thought I might be fired.

The CEO was, however, relieved of his position. We came to learn that the board had held an extraordinary meeting the day before to review the performance of the company but found out that not much progress had been made in six months. The board deliberated and concluded that the problem with the company was not the staff but the CEO's style of leadership, and so they decided to let him go.

They appointed an acting CEO whose first task was to compile a list of staff who had consistently exceeded their KPIs and who qualified for a promotion. That was how I was promoted on the day I expected to be fired. I worked for another six years in that company. Things turned around. I got a mortgage to buy my first house, and I had several opportunities to develop myself even further. I left only when the shareholders sold the company.

Life Lessons

1. **Every seed has a harvest.** My former boss wanted me fired and listed me as a nonperformer. Unfortunately, he ended up being fired. Do not do evil to others. What we do has a way of coming back to us. If you sow good seeds, you will reap a good harvest. Conversely if you sow evil seeds, you will likely reap the same.

2. **Pleasant surprises still happen.** My prayer was to retain my job, but my expectation was exceeded. I was promoted on the day I thought I might be fired. If you are at the valley of your life now, don't give up. Remain hopeful. Pleasant surprises still happen. Remain optimistic. Every problem has an expiration date.

Uncommon Promotion

I was the branch manager of a company in the mid-nineties, and our performance was excellent. Due to the high performance, the board of directors decided to host their board meeting outside the corporate head office and in our city.

During that board meeting, one of the items discussed was staff promotion. Everyone assumed I would be promoted, but I wasn't. Later, one of the directors who was close to me had to ask me if there was a personal issue between me and the CEO. I told him there wasn't. The reason he asked was because my name came up for promotion, but the CEO mentioned that even though I met the requirements they should stay action for now. The board deferred to him, while I kept working as hard as I could.

Exactly one year later, another board meeting took place at the corporate head office. The CEO recommended that I be promoted retroactively with effect from the previous year. I benefitted from a one-year incremental salary and bonus. I can't explain why the decision was made, but I was glad and grateful to enjoy the benefits.

Life Lessons

1. **Never grumble.** I imagine that the CEO was assessing my capacity for leadership, as the promotion would place me in a senior management cadre. I was not demotivated by the delay; neither did I grumble or complain. In fact, I went on with my job as if nothing had happened. I must have passed the unwritten test, and one year later, I was rewarded.

   When things are not going your way, take it in good spirits. Understand that management has the discretion to make the decisions they believe are best. That's why they are in leadership. Stop complaining and keep working.

2. **Keep confidential information confidential.** When that director confided in me, he expected me to keep the information to myself, and I did. When you are entrusted with confidential information, keep it to yourself. You will not get future information if you cannot carefully keep the information available to you.

3. **Don't be discouraged.** When I missed that promotion, I could have been discouraged, and that would have adversely affected my performance. Although I was not happy when the promotion list was released, I didn't let it affect my job.

Taking Up Opportunities

I worked in many different companies as a young man. I changed jobs at the slightest opportunity. I worked with foreign and local organizations, with exposure to the best global banking principles. My colleagues and I walked tall and looked smart.

Despite this, I woke up one day and resigned from one of the great jobs. I resigned for two reasons: I got a better offer, and I had received shocking treatment from the head of human resources, a member of the executive management team. I had just qualified as a chartered accountant and, with excitement, I had approached him to break the good news. He listened while I spoke and then asked me to leave his office if that was all I had to say. I was shocked by this treatment and immediately began searching for another job.

Shortly thereafter, I got another banking job. At that time, I was an assistant manager, single, well-paid, and in my late twenties. In the new organization, I immediately noticed unhealthy rivalry and acrimony among the non-executive directors. Trouble was brewing, and I could see that the future of the bank was in doubt. I worked there for only nine months and left.

I moved on to another bank. This bank was owned by a business mogul and was professionally run. I worked in this bank for ten years.

Life Lessons

1. **Take risks when you are young.** Changing jobs where necessary is part of taking risks. Explore new offers and meet new people, especially before you have a family. If you don't do this when you are young, you may regret it when you get old. I am glad I took those risks, and most of them paid off.

2. **Never trade off a great brand without compensation.**
While working with the local subsidiary of an American bank, I was equipped with skills sufficient to work anywhere in the world. The brand was attached to my name. When I was negotiating for another job with an unknown brand, I insisted on being compensated for trading off that brand. I insisted on two grade levels above my level. I got it. Don't trade off a good brand associated with you without adequate compensation.

3. **Some executives do not realize the power of their words.**
Senior people in organizations must carefully choose their words, most especially if they are in human resources. I expected a commendation from HR for acquiring skills at my own expense that would ultimately benefit the bank, but I received the opposite. The higher you go, the more careful you need to be with your words.

4. **Look into the future.** When working at an organization, always consider its long-term sustainability. If it does not have a long-term outlook, don't tie your destiny to it. Immediately upon joining the second bank and noticing the level of acrimony among the directors, I knew the bank did not have a future. So I took courage and left. That was one of the best decisions of my banking career.

Chapter 7

Training Stories

I believe in continuous training and education. Formal education is wonderful, but it is not sufficient for facing challenges in a fast-changing world. I kept pursuing training in professional accountancy, business leadership, and spiritual development. Some of the training took me to other countries in search of knowledge and to ensure my technical capacity remained top-notch.

I have many stories along the lines of education and training. Here are some of them.

Best and Brightest Bankers

Many years ago, I had a neighbor who I will call Mrs T (not her real name) who kept praying for me and encouraging me to draw closer to God. I really was not interested. I moved to Port Harcourt, but she did not give up on me in prayers. Today, as a result of her prayers, I am a minister of God.

Mrs T called me from Lagos to tell me she had visited her brother and overheard her sister-in-law, a banker, lamenting over an application form. She had gotten a form to apply for a special program organized by the United States Agency for International Development (USAID). It was for training of the smartest African bankers in the United States on full scholarship for six weeks. Funding was approved by Congress. Five people were to be selected from Nigeria and twenty-six altogether from Africa.

Her sister-in-law had taken the application form to her boss for his endorsement. Instead of agreeing to do so, the boss asked her to give him the form to apply for himself. The lady was angry and was about to tear up the form rather than surrender it to her boss. It was at this point Mrs T intervened and asked her to give the form to me.

I got the form and quickly completed it. The next hurdle was getting my managing director in Lagos to recommend me and agree to release me for six weeks. Thankfully, he made an unscheduled visit to Port Harcourt and gladly approved the training program.

I was offered the scholarship. I had been chosen as one of Africa's best and brightest bankers to be trained by USAID. The package came with a round-trip ticket, free hotel accommodation for six weeks, and several other incidental expenses.

The training itself was detailed and comprehensive. It covered stints in several top American banks and the government in Washington, DC. We had amazing technical and practical trainings. The exposure was a once-in-a-lifetime experience. What I learned helped to shape my entire banking career. It was an amazing networking experience, too. I still feel deeply grateful to the US government for the rare gesture.

Life Lessons

1. **Maintain healthy relationships.** My relationship with my former neighbor opened the door for this opportunity. It was because we had a great relationship that she thought of me. God blesses people through people. Nurture and maintain relationships. I am forever grateful to her for that favor. I am still nurturing that relationship. Nurture yours.

2. **Every drama has a purpose.** The disagreement between my friend's sister-in-law and her boss had a purpose. Their disagreement was a blessing to me. It looked like a drama, but if that boss had signed the application, there would be no story like this to tell.

   Have you asked yourself why my friend's sister-in-law was lamenting about the experience at home? Why was she also saying it at the time my friend visited her brother? Why was she threatening to tear up the application form at home? Why did she not tear it up at the office? Why did she not consider going back to appeal to her boss to change his mind? Why did she freely release the form? There is someone who rules the affairs of men. It appears as a drama, but it was divinely orchestrated.

3. **Never give up.** I was extremely worried about the short time for the submission of that form. If my CEO had not unexpectedly visited, there would have been no way for me to meet the deadline for submission. Just before I lost hope, God intervened. That singular visit by my CEO changed the course of history in my favor.

   Never lose hope on any matter. Keep working, but at the same time, keep hoping against hope. Help will come when you least expect it.

First-Time Author

I was originally a science student who loved history. I knew I was not a literary giant. I lacked the literary skills to write for mass readership. I believed my village upbringing and attendance at rural schools were limiting me mentally. I never dreamed of being an author. I believed that authors were a special breed of people born to write.

But then I became a preacher, and at some point, I was inspired

Simon Aranonu

to write the weekly church bulletin. It was a two-page bulletin that summarized the sermon I had preached the previous Sunday, along with prayer points and a few announcements of birthdays and church programs. I summoned a lot of courage to write that bulletin, which I called *Solution News*.

To my utter surprise, complimentary remarks started flowing from different directions, including the church members, on the quality of the content. I did not take their compliments seriously, because I thought they might be patronizing me. My disposition changed when nonmembers and my wife, my main critic, also complimented the bulletin.

Three years later, I was strongly inspired to convert the two-page bulletin into a full-fledged magazine. I gathered seven other respected authors as contributors on different subthemes. I shared my vision with them, and a brand-new sixteen-page color magazine called *Solution News* was born. That was December 2009. For the next ten years, that monthly magazine was in publication, selling in large quantities. We later changed the name to *Breakthrough*. Again, complimentary feedback flowed in. My confidence soared. Not only could I write, but I could proofread what the contributing editors wrote.

Then one day, I heard a voice inside me saying, *It's time to write a book*. This didn't have to be a brand-new book; I was just to compile all the articles I had written over the years and rearrange them along themes, and a book would be born. I did just that, and *Solution Capsules* was published in 2019. The book sold over ten thousand copies within a year. I also had a Spanish edition published two years after or in the year 2021. The feedback and market response have been humbling. And here we are today, with you reading my third book.

Life Lessons

1. **Every big thing starts small.** When I started a two-page weekly bulletin, I didn't know it would mark the birth of a book that would be sold globally. I started small but kept being inspired. Do not despise the days of humble beginnings, and be patient. Certainly, every good thing takes time to grow.

2. **Whatever you do, do it well.** I took my time when writing my articles. Some were written late into the quiet night; some were written inside aircrafts when I had a long journey ahead of me; others were written while I was on vacation. Whenever I felt inspired, I wrote. I also took time to proofread over and over to ensure the quality was good. I was afraid of failure and came out with quality write-ups each time.

    There is potential in you. I didn't know I could write or produce a reader-friendly document. I didn't know the potential was there. It only needed to be stirred by the fan of encouraging words.

    You will be amazed at what you can do. Your potential is great. Your installed capacity is less than 10 percent utilized. Believe in yourself. Ignore voices inside you that keep telling you that you are not good enough. Those voices spoke to me constantly but were silenced.

    Silence any voice telling you that you are not good. Believe the lone gentle voice asking you to try. It is the voice of possibility. Even if you try and fail, keep trying. You will one day play on the global stage, if only you believe.

1. **Think big.** A person can hardly achieve beyond what he is able to imagine or think. As a man thinks, so he will be. The mind can limit you if you don't engage it to think big. From the day I started putting the book together, I

decided to publish a book that the whole world would read. I chose to use a reputable global book publisher in America rather than local publishers. I also wanted my book listed on Amazon immediately. In my mind, I was seeing my book displayed in bookstores all over the world.

2. **Expand your thinking capacity.** You may have been born and raised in a poor rural background like mine. But you should not remain there. Your mind is not rural or poor. Get liberated in the mind. In your small corner, begin to think global.

Professional Certified Accountant

My undergraduate degree was in finance. I admired chartered accountants, but since my undergraduate degree was not in accounting, I initially did not bother to toe this professional line. Additionally, I heard scary stories of how difficult and challenging it was to qualify as a chartered accountant. The institute also had a limited number of students who could qualify each year. But after a while, it became my dream to qualify as a chartered accountant.

I enrolled in a tutorial college that prepared candidates for professional examinations. I wrote my first professional-level examination, and for the first time in my life, I failed woefully. This shook and humbled me. I had to retake the examination at the next session. I kept progressing until I got to the final professional level.

I was told the real battle is at the final qualifying exams. I was a young bank officer extremely busy in the office and needed time to study and prepare. I decided to apply for my annual vacation to enable me to prepare for exams.

A day from the end of my two weeks' vacation, the deputy head of my unit in the office, Aunty Mo, visited me at home. She asked me two questions: "Have you covered the syllabus? Do you feel ready?" I confessed that I was not ready. She left my apartment and promised to do something about it.

The next day, I was granted an additional two weeks to prepare for the exams. Those extra two weeks were worth more than a million dollars. By the time I walked into the examination hall, I knew I was ready. I passed the examination and qualified that same year as a chartered accountant.

Life Lessons

1. **Anything is possible.** Whatever you set your mind to do, keep at it, and you will one day succeed. I was initially scared about attempting the exams when I heard stories of woes from those who tried and failed. Although I was terrified at the outset, I later conquered my fears. I made up my mind to give it my best shot. I fought hard. I worked hard. I was determined to succeed. It shut me out of the social scene for two years as I attended intensive all-weekend preparatory tutorials. Many times, I slept over in the classrooms, studying late into the night. I was twenty-seven and single. It was worth the sacrifice.

2. **Failure is normal.** Since I had never failed a major examination before this, failure at the first professional level was a rude shock. But then I decided to see failure as a wakeup call to work even harder and be more determined. No one who has ever succeeded in life does not have stories of previous failures.

3. **You need an angel.** Aunty Mo was my angel for the qualifying exams. I feel indebted to her for life. Providence was at work for her to visit me that day and subsequently assist in obtaining an extension of my vacation. In life, you need an angel like Aunty Mo. I don't know how to get such unsolicited helpers of destiny. But I believe that if you are

hardworking and humble, providence will arrange your own Aunty Mo for you.

Business School

Some years ago, I had this hunger to study in an Ivy League business school in the United States. I identified the leadership program I wanted and sought my CEO's consent. I had five months to prepare. I made sure my visa was up to date. My boss gave me his word in April, and the training was to be held in August.

In the intervening period, a few developments took place in the office, and all overseas training was suspended. So I didn't bother to apply for the program.

Early in August, the circumstances that had led to the suspension of overseas training changed. I went back to the CEO to seek his approval for the training, and he asked me to confirm whether the application date was still open. The following day, I got a response with apologies that admissions into the program had closed but that I would be placed on a waiting list. I was seventh on the waiting list, but if any confirmed admitted potential students dropped off, I would be considered. I did my calculations, and the possibility seemed near zero.

Then, three days before the commencement of training, I received a letter offering me admission. The offer was predicated on my acceptance of same within twenty-four hours. I immediately accepted the offer, and my office effected remittance of the training fees. The following day, I was on my way to the United States on a fourteen-hour flight.

I arrived around two in the afternoon on the day before the training commenced. Though very exhausted, I was still part of the early arrivals and joined the welcome cocktail and introductory formalities.

During lunch break the next day, the program coordinator

came looking for me. She gave me a bear hug and said she wanted to meet the miracle man from Africa. According to her, my being part of the program was nothing short of a miracle. Four days before the commencement of training, one previously confirmed and admitted person called to cancel. It had been her responsibility to reach out to all those on the waiting list in the queue order. All six of the people ahead of me turned down the offer, since the time was short. She was pleasantly surprised that the last man she contacted, from another continent, accepted, paid, and arrived for class well ahead of some others.

Life Lessons

1. **Be prepared always.** It was a good thing that my visa to the United States was current and I was mentally prepared for the trip. I encourage you to always keep your valid travel, statutory, and personal documents up to date. You don't know when these documents will be required at short notice.
2. **If you fail, try again.** When the CEO suspended approvals for foreign training, I still believed that the suspension would be lifted one day. It took four months for this to happen, and I was on the alert. Always remain positive. Delay is not denial.
3. **Miracles still happen.** The training coordinator described my arrival in the program as a miracle. I didn't stand much of a chance as number seven on the waiting list. But it happened. Try not to figure out how things will work out for you. Your duty is to do what you need to do and expect the best. I believe in miracles. Miracles still happen.

Journey in Accountancy

I studied finance in university and didn't initially plan to become a chartered accountant. However, in the first three years on campus, students studying for a first degree in accountancy, finance, business management, and marketing interacted a lot due to the similarity in our courses and because we were all in the faculty.

I recall that one of the students was not particularly smart and graduated with a third-class degree. Four years after graduation, this guy was one of the first to qualify as a chartered accountant. His success was one of the things that spurred me into attempting the examination.

But there were many obstacles for me, especially with the availability of time and money. Tutorial classes, books, and examination fees were expensive. My meagre salary could not foot those bills. So I went searching for a primary school friend who had become a successful trader. He avoided me by giving me appointments but not showing up for them. After a while, I gave up on trying to speak with him.

I turned to another friend, Caesar, who was then working in a merchant bank and had qualified as an accountant. He lent me the money immediately. That was how I enrolled in the tutorials and examination. May God bless Caesar.

Time was a major constraint, too, because I was working full-time in banking and writing a highly demanding examination at the same time. However, this was resolved by one of my supervisors providing support with extra vacation days. In addition to this, I made the best use of the time I had.

Life Lessons

1. **Be steadfast.** When you set a clear goal, there will always be resources required to achieve it. In my own case,

money and time were limiting factors. But I refused to give up. I kept trying. When one of my childhood friends disappointed me, I tried another.

Never give up when you need something, no matter the frustrations. Successful people never give up. Even when they fail, they try again.

2. **Time is money.** It's a miracle how I juggled so many balls at the same time without dropping any. Banking is a strenuous occupation. The demand on my time was huge. Preparing to qualify for a professional accountancy exam was time-demanding. It was like holding two full-time jobs at the same time. Notwithstanding, I was able to handle both effectively. Do not waste time. Time is more than money.

3. **Never look down on people.** The person I considered not quite smart in university qualified as a chartered accountant ahead of me. Pride is not good. When that fellow qualified, I was challenged. Stop looking at history alone to determine success.

Many university mates who did not excel academically have done extremely well post-graduation. Many have gotten ahead by working extra-hard to improve on their academic credentials. They may have conquered new territories. The person you think would be a nobody may be your boss tomorrow.

Leave the past in the past where it belongs. If you do not move as quickly as possible, the guys you thought you left behind yesterday may leave you behind tomorrow.

One-Star, Double-Star

In times past, the Institute of Chartered Accountants of Nigeria (ICAN) had three qualifying levels of examinations. Naturally, if you passed one level, you could progress to the next until you passed the final qualifying exam.

Failing the exams had unique reprimands. If you scored slightly below passing, you would be awarded what was called a *one star* in that subject. If you earn a one star in not more than two subjects (meaning you comfortably passed the rest), you would be given the opportunity to retake the one-star papers during the next exam period. If, however, your failure rate was way below the pass mark, you would be awarded a *double star*. A double star in one subject was a technical failure of all the other subjects, and the student would have to retake all at the next exam period. It was therefore basic wisdom to avoid a double star like the plague.

I had just bagged a bachelor's degree, graduating at the top of my class. Considering that I had attended a relatively unknown missionary high school, excelling against students from better schools made me think I was a star. I became proud.

Then I enrolled in an ICAN tutorial college. I registered to write the ICAN professional qualifying exams. Notwithstanding that I borrowed money from my friend to pay for the tutorials, I didn't put in enough effort. I barely attended classes or did my assignments. My confidence was based on my assessment of my intelligence and competence. I had proved it before; I would prove it again.

I wrote the ICAN exams. In those days, exam results were always posted on the notice board of the institute. Those who were not sure of good scores would either go to check their results when there were few people around or ask their friends to check for them. With hands in my pockets, I arrogantly and majestically approached the notice board. To my shock, I had earned a double star in two subjects. I called a guy nearby to help me confirm it. By this time, my legs were wobbly, and I was seeing stars. With head bowed, I walked out of the ICAN office feeling badly disgraced.

To add salt to my injury, I saw others celebrating with drinks.

Incidentally, many of the guys I had looked down on did well. I went into a period of introspection and told myself the truth. I was singularly responsible for what had befallen me.

I dusted myself off and re-enrolled in the tutorial college. I fired on all cylinders, as I used to do on campus. I passed the exams at the next sitting and eventually became a chartered accountant.

ICAN didn't just teach me accounting; it also taught me humility. I was humiliated before I learned humility. When people see me today and say I am humble, I laugh. I did not willingly become humble. ICAN forced it on me.

Life Lessons

1. **Don't be proud.** Do not learn the hard way like me. If I was not proud, I could have passed those exams in one sitting, possibly with awards. A popular British proverb says "pride goes before a fall."

2. **When you have new problems, remember the weapons you used before that gave you victory.** Those weapons will work again. If I had applied myself with diligence as I did on campus, I would not have suffered disgrace. If prayer vigils or praise worked for you before, use them again to confront the current problems you are facing.

3. **When you are down, don't give up.** God always leaves room for another chance. You may be down, but you are not out. Do not throw in the towel. You have not been counted out. You are still in the boxing ring. Get up and fight.

   I'm grateful I tried the exams again. No matter how down you are now, get up and try again. I am confident you will still win. God will help you. The fact that you are still alive means you can still get up. You can still make it. I am confident that I will soon hear your testimonies.

Chapter 8

Travel and Tours

I love traveling and meeting new people from different races and countries. I see myself as a global citizen. I have visited most continents of the world and would love to visit more countries, especially places of unique interests.

I am expectant each time I travel because from experience, I usually meet people whose lives I transform and vice versa. Here are some of my travel stories to inspire you.

Pay as You Eat

Many years ago, when I made my first trip out of Africa to America to attend a credit school at Citi Bank in New York, I commuted from New Jersey daily for weeks by train and at some point, met another Nigerian called Ade. I also made friends with some Americans, and we often hung out together during lunch breaks.

On the first Friday of the training, two of my American friends invited me for a drink at the bar of the Empire State Building, which had a full view of New York City. I gladly accepted the invitation and invited Ade to tag along. My friends invited another friend of theirs.

We had a good time drinking and eating snacks. Finally, it

was time to go; I needed to catch my train back to New Jersey. I was getting ready to thank them for the gesture when a surprise developed: each of my American friends mentioned the number of nuts they ate and the value of their drinks. Each one in turn dropped dollar bills to cover what he ate or drank. I was in shock. In Africa, when you invite someone for a drink, it's implied that you will pick up the bill.

I only had my ticket money to New Jersey—no credit card. I signaled to Ade and expressed my shock. Thankfully, Ade had some extra cash. He bailed me out. I shook hands with my new friends with a fake smile. Our friendship did not go beyond that weekend. I declined subsequent invitations for outings. I never understood the culture. I just felt the guys were being mean. How wrong I was in my judgements.

Life Lessons

1. **Don't make friends in a hurry.** Take time to understand people before you befriend them. Practice courtship before you cement a friendship. Ensure you have agreements on a few critical lifestyle issues before you plunge into the friendship and begin to reveal your secrets.

2. **Don't walk alone.** I survived embarrassment that night because I had Ade with me. He rescued me. Partnership helps. You need an Ade to accompany you. It's called *synergy*. It's the power of two.

3. **Take responsibility.** On due reflection, I wonder why I expected my new friends to pick up my bill. They were not Santa Claus. We'd just met. Why should they start the friendship with a financial loss? Be ready to pay for what you want. If you cannot afford it, wait until you can. Nothing is free. Someone must pay for something before you have it.

4. **Don't think for your friends.** I assumed that those guys would pay my bill. I was basically thinking for them. But nobody knows what's in a man's heart. Think for yourself. At best, ask questions. If I had asked my new friends who would pay the bill, I would not have been embarrassed. Stop making assumptions for your friends. You will have fewer conflicts if you talk things over.

5. **Don't judge another person's culture.** I made a mistake that day by thinking the culture of my American friends was the same as mine. I was naïve and wrong. I should not have used my own culture as a benchmark. No culture is superior or inferior to another. It takes understanding and accommodation to live happily together. We are all uniquely made. Our strength lies in our diversity.

6. **Don't go out without money.** This advice may sound funny, but don't go out without cash or cards. You may have a flat tire if you are driving. An emergency may come up. I struggle with heeding this advice myself, and my wife has bailed me out countless times.

7. **Do not be quick to accept invitations.** I wish I had pondered more deeply before I accepted that invitation to the Empire State Building. I acted on impulse; we all do. If I'd reflected deeply, I would have assessed my wallet. Imagine what would have happened if Ade could not bail me out? Always plan and reflect deeply before you make critical decisions. That way, you will not repeat the mistakes I made.

Embassies and Visas

Some years ago, my employers recommended me for a training program in a foreign bank. I had never traveled outside the country before that. With absolutely no documentation, I attended the interview, and to my shock, my visa application was turned down.

I was a manager in a bank. I had a good job. I had no intention of relocating abroad. I wished the interviewers would see my mind.

I reapplied for the visa, this time with loads of documents and a direct invitation letter from the foreign bank. When I approached the consular officer, however, he asked me only one question: "The training has started, and even if you travel today, you will only attend half of the training. What do you intend to do?" I was so upset by the question. In my mind, I blamed the embassy for the delay. I told him not to bother about the visa any longer. He saw my disappointment, but he also saw my integrity.

To my surprise, he decided there and then to give me a two-year multiple visa so I could attend the program any time it came up again in the future.

Thirty years later, and after several visits to that country, my visa application was rejected again. When I went for the repeat visa interview, the lady just asked me to name all the companies I'd worked for over the years. I listed them. Then she asked if I was the one who completed my application form. I told her no; my personal assistant did, because I am a busy person.

That was when she informed me that the electronic application form contained only information about my present employment and nothing about any previous employment. I was in shock. I didn't know my integrity was being tested. I just said the truth. She could see my integrity, however. She asked me to include all the information on my employment records and granted me the visa.

Life Lessons

1. **Countries usually welcome genuine visitors.** Every country loves visitors, especially because of the attendant funds inflow, which will have a positive impact on their

economy. However, no country wants illegal immigrants. If you can show that you are on a legitimate mission, they will gladly welcome you to their country.

2. **Be prepared.** If you attend a visa interview, make sure you are prepared and have all the required documents. My first application would not have failed if I had attended with sufficient documentation. It's your responsibility to prove to the consular officer that your trip is genuine and that you have enough ties to your country to ensure your return.

3. **There is no shortcut to proper review.** Responsibility and ownership become yours whenever you append your signature. Being a busy executive was no excuse for my grievous error. This was resolved easily, but similar errors could end up with far-reaching consequences that could have been avoided.

4. **Integrity has no alternative.** One key test you must pass to get a visa is the test of integrity. Understand that you have no reason to lie. Be honest. Answer every question honestly. It's often easy for the consular officer to sense if you are lying. The truth will save you headaches and heartaches.

5. **Follow due process.** What many people do not know is that every country has a legitimate process for admitting legal immigrants. If you want to immigrate to any country, follow due process. Find out if you are qualified. Do the right thing. Do not attempt to obtain a tourist visa with the intention of living in that country. That will make you an illegal immigrant, and that's fraud.

Pilgrimage

At one time, I did not have a regular job and was living hand-to-mouth. My only trip out of the country in five years was to two

West African countries, Ghana and Gambia. Both were on teaching trips sponsored by the training organization I worked with.

But even though I was low on finances, I made a ten-day pilgrimage to Israel, organized by the Redeemed Christian Church of God. Miraculously, I received a phone call from a former member of my church who had relocated to another country. He offered to sponsor the trip for my wife and me and to cover tickets and spending allowance. It was like a dream, but it was also a memorable pleasant surprise.

During the trip, we couldn't help but pray for our friend every day that God would bless him abundantly. His wife was awaiting some immigration approvals. We prayed that God would intervene, and within a few weeks after the pilgrimage, the papers were approved.

Another remarkable thing happened on the trip. My wife owned and managed a small store in our gated community. She met one of her customers on that pilgrimage. My wife said hello, but the woman ignored her and walked away. My wife couldn't understand why, but she put the incident behind her.

Weeks later, when we were back in Lagos, the same woman showed up in her store. She warmed up and smiled at my wife. My wife asked why she had been so cold in Israel while extending such warm felicitations in Lagos. The lady almost had a heart attack. She confessed that she could not reconcile the poor woman in the store with the woman she met in Israel. She apologized profusely.

Life Lessons

1. **What you sow is what you reap.** Because that man blessed me by sponsoring the trip, my wife and I entreated heaven for ten days for the needs of his family. We asked God to give them what money cannot buy. Be careful to do good

to as many people as possible. The good or evil that people do is often multiplied and returned to them.

2. **Miracles still happen.** Never give up on yourself. God is still an expert in reversing the irreversible and turning hopeless cases around. When I least expected this trip to Israel, I made it. Please remain optimistic. Do not ever consider giving up. Help may be on the way. And it may come from sources you don't expect.

3. **Don't judge people by their appearance.** That woman judged my wife by her location and appearance. She profiled her mentally and put her in a box. Please don't form a conclusive opinion of anyone based on what you see so you don't make grievous mistakes.

I Will Escort You

I was in Philadelphia attending a five-week training program for African bankers sponsored by the USAID. I had a friend in Stroudsburg and decided to spend the weekend with him. I needed to catch a bus but wasn't quite sure of the directions.

I got the attention of a lady near the station who calmly stopped to listen to me and gave me directions to the bus station. I turned, but then she offered to show me the way. As we walked along, we got to talking. She seemed quite excited to learn that I was a pastor and a banker.

Finally, it was my turn to ask questions. I was excited to learn that she was from Ogun state, Nigeria. She wanted me to pray for her and asked for my contact details.

She came to see me shortly afterward and asked me to pray that God would send her a husband so she could get married. We prayed, and I shared my Nigerian phone number with her.

On my return to Nigeria, she called me and shared her testimony. A few days after our prayers, she received a phone call from an old schoolmate from the University of Lagos. The man straight away asked if she would consider marrying him. She traveled to Nigeria so they could meet properly, and soon enough, they were married.

Life Lessons

1. **Do not be afraid to ask for help.** Some are too proud to ask for help and could be headed in the wrong direction without knowing it. If I hadn't asked for help, I could have missed my bus.

2. **Be courteous and hospitable.** The lady was unusually hospitable. She went out of her way to help a stranger. She not only provided direction but also showed me the way. When you are helping strangers, you may be helping an angel sent to help *you*. Be courteous always. You don't know when and how God wants to do a miracle.

3. **Capture opportunities when you have them.** Critical lifetime opportunities do not come up every day. When you have them, capture and maximize them. The moment she found out I was a preacher, she asked for a prayer. Her door opened in less than three days.

Preaching Trip

I was working and living in Lagos when one day I was invited to preach in Port Harcourt. It was a forty-five-minute flight. I had a return ticket, as I needed to fly back immediately to be at work in Lagos the next day. The last flight back to Lagos would leave at two thirty Sunday afternoon.

We had an excellent Sunday service. Many people needed my attention, and by the time I left the church, it was already about two in the afternoon. We sped off to the airport and arrived there at a few minutes before three.

I went straight to the check-in counter and presented my ticket, but I was politely told that check-in had closed, all passengers had boarded, and the plane was about to taxi off. After a few minutes of chatting, however, the staff at the check-in counter told me something unusual in aviation practice was happening: the pilot had left the aircraft for over fifteen minutes in the same position on the runway without moving.

As soon as I heard this, I asked them for a favor. I asked them to issue me a boarding pass. They did and allowed me to go and try my luck. I ran to the tarmac and waved my boarding pass. The pilot saw me and asked the crew to open the door of the plane for me. They did, and I boarded.

Immediately, I put on my seat belt, and the pilot announced to the passengers that the plane was now ready for takeoff. I could hear passengers grumbling and hissing. Some thought I was a prominent VIP and was the reason for the delay. Some were angry that the pilot didn't apologize to them. I stayed cool, grateful that I would be in the office in good time the next day.

Life Lessons

1. **Nothing ends until God says so.** That flight was obviously delayed because of me, though the pilot did not know what he was doing. I believe in God. I believe there is One who rules in the affairs of men. Nothing is an accident with God. He knows everything before it happens. If you do your own bit, the one who controls the affairs of men may influence things to favor you.

2. **Keep trying.** When I arrived at the airport and was told that the plane had boarded, the natural reaction would have been to return to my hotel room and bemoan my situation. But I refused to do that. I kept smiling and chatting with the guys at the counter. I asked about the

status of the plane. My subtle pressure made them check what was happening and even issue me a boarding pass. Whatever happens, despite the obstacles, just keep trying!

Visiting Aunty Mo

Aunty Mo is my mentor and friend. We met in 1988 when I got employed at the then Continental Merchant Bank (CMB). CMB was a subsidiary of Chase Manhattan Bank. It was previously called Chase Merchant Bank. Aunty Mo was a friend from day one. She was caring. She was humble. She was patient in teaching. She taught me banking.

Three years later, we both had left CMB to work in different banks. But our friendship grew deeper, and very soon (and still) I had become her "brother from another mother." Aunty Mo paid for my wedding rings thirty years ago. On that same wedding day, she gladly released her new Honda Accord to be used to drive my wife to the wedding. The first television set I ever owned was Aunty Mo's.

When I did not have a job, she gladly got me into her training firm, where I stayed for nearly seven years. When I faced a potential financial mess and my creditor bank was about to foreclose on my property, Aunty Mo intervened immediately, and the bank delivered a pleasant surprise, including partial but massively substantial debt forgiveness. The list is literally endless of the blessings I have received through Aunty Mo.

When she fell sick in London, I would lose sleep praying most nights for her recovery. Finally, it was time for me to visit her in London. I did not have details about the hospital. I did not have her home address. I did not know where I was going. I only had a phone number. It was an anxious trip.

I arrived in London after an all-night six-hour flight. When I was at immigration, the gentleman asked, "What brought you to London?"

I quickly answered, "I've come to see my friend and ex-boss who is also my 'sister from another mother.'"

The immigration officer asked if I knew how she paid her medical bills. I said I did not know. He asked if I knew the hospital. I said I did not. He asked if I knew whether she was in a residence or hospital. I said I did not know. He asked if I knew her residential address. I said I did not know.

I told the immigration officer that I had a phone number, and that I was confident that when I got her on the phone, she would describe where she was. He asked me how long I would stay in London. I answered, "Twenty-four hours." He let me in.

It was as I was passing through immigration that I realized how stupid I was. How could I leave one continent for another without knowing exactly where I was going? I only booked a hotel for myself. However, on reflection, I knew that the immigration officer could see the integrity on my face. He could see an honesty that covered my stupidity.

I eventually met my friend. She is well and back now. My anxiety and stupidity are over. I give glory to God.

Life Lessons

1. **Some friends are like blood relatives.** I thank God for the day I met Aunty Mo. She has played critical roles in my life, and she still does. What started as an office boss-to-staff relationship has blossomed into an extended family relationship. It's been thirty-three years and still counting. She assisted me in becoming a chartered accountant (certified public accountant). My children call her aunty. She is a friend to my wife. Both families are integrated and interwoven.

Cultivate healthy clean relationships. When properly handled, some may grow into lifelong relationships that could rank on the same level as blood relatives.

2. **Honesty covers stupidity.** The UK immigration officer could see through my eyes of integrity, even as he saw my stupidity or naivety. When you are telling the truth, people know. I always counsel young people about traveling abroad. I tell them that every country wants to receive visitors. You will spend your money in their country in addition to flying on their airline. Every country you visit, you actually make richer by your trip.

Countries want to encourage visitors. But they are looking for honest and genuine visitors who will complete their visits and go back home. Be honest when you visit countries. The immigration officers have been trained. They can sort through the rubble. Even if you are stupid, your honesty will cover your stupidity.

Finally, on the Pandemic (COVID-19)

In the last quarter of 2019, news evolved about a strange disease that many people assumed would soon be under control like other outbreaks before it. The world was not ready for what was to come. The disease spread far and wide and soon became an official global pandemic. Many countries were on lockdown, and I felt the need to make videos to encourage people all over the world as they tried to cope with this global crisis.

To date, millions of lives have been lost globally to this pandemic. Thankfully, vaccines have been made. I quickly got vaccinated and encouraged others around me to do the same.

At some point, I had to travel out of the country and did the mandatory preflight COVID test. I tested negative before I traveled out and had the same result before I boarded my return flight. Back in Nigeria, I complied with the government regulations and isolated myself for seven days, after which I took the final flight-related mandatory COVID-19 test.

However, and unfortunately, this time I had a positive test result. My hands trembled as I reviewed the report. I advised my wife to move to another room immediately, as I had to quarantine myself. Fear and anxiety set in.

I called my senior pastors and asked them to pray. I spoke with my doctor, who advised me to buy an oximeter immediately while he began to manage me from home. My symptoms were mild, and I was advised to call the hospital immediately if I had respiratory problems.

Thankfully, I did not develop respiratory problems, but I needed emotional and spiritual support. My senior pastors prayed, while relatives, colleagues, and friends provided emotional support.

My wife stood by me like a pillar as usual. She slept on the couch in the living room nearby just in case I had a crisis in the night. Thank God there was none. I often heard her constant prayers. She took time to provide all kinds of healthy meals, fruits, and vegetables while also speaking with me on the phone consistently. I'm grateful that she was not infected. May God bless my wife.

I was on analgesics, but that didn't keep the fever under control. Having taken the permissible maximum dose, I reverted to my doctors. One of them recommended what he called "wet towel therapy." This involved soaking a towel in cold water and pressing it on the body to bring down the temperature. It worked. I did that for several nights and took all my vitamins and recommended drugs even though they were just palliatives. I understood that clearly.

I prayed as much as I could. A few friends kept checking on me, while others who couldn't were probably also busy with their own issues. Two weeks after I did the first test, I was still positive and felt bad, even though I was happy that all other medical tests showed no permanent damage to my health.

Exactly twenty-four days afterward, I tested negative for the virus and was declared healthy. My anxiety fizzled away, and my blood pressure normalized. What can be a better relief than being declared healed of a disease that has no medical cure? My joy knew no bounds. I am eternally grateful to God that I am alive to tell this story.

Life Lessons

1. **Obey government rules.** I am grateful that I complied with the government rules on quarantine. This protected my family members and helped in the early detection when I went for the post-arrival test within seven days. Please take a cue from this and ensure you always comply with positive government guidelines. The guidelines are for your benefit and for the benefit of others in your country.

2. **Get vaccinated.** I know God gave me a healing miracle. I've heard of people who got fully vaccinated but still died of COVID-19. However, I also believe my full vaccination helped me tremendously. It obviously helped in mitigating the potential damage that could have occurred. Please get fully vaccinated, and don't be careless.

3. **People are busy.** The world is not about you alone. I've observed that my wife is the most reliable constant factor in my life outside of God. Colleagues are busy. Friends and family are occupied with their lives. Don't take offence if they don't get back to check on you, and don't expect too much. Forgive any perceived offense and move on.

4. **Obey your doctor.** I obeyed all the instructions from my doctor, and that helped. Obeying your doctor is not optional. If your doctor asks you to stop smoking, to stop taking certain foods, or to take certain medications, please obey. It's all for your good.

5. **Life goes on.** My twenty-four-day isolation taught me a few deep lessons, some of which I am sharing here. I was alone in a room for twenty-four days, with no TV or social media and no physical interaction with friends or office and church colleagues.

During this time, I pondered on how all the things we pursue in life will no longer matter one day. I thought about what will happen when I leave this planet. On that day, it will be me alone, just like the twenty-four days of isolation. What will matter then will be only the life hereafter.

Are you prepared for life after here? Do you know where you are headed when you transit out of this earth? If you are sure, I congratulate you. If you are not sure of where you will go when you die, and you want to open a discussion about that with me, I will be glad to assist. You can reach me at simonaranonu@gmail.com.

God bless you. I will soon read about your testimonies.

Conclusion

Everyone's stories is unique. It can be challenging to recollect lifetime stories after many decades and to tell them without reservation. I am grateful to God that I can recollect these stories and now share them with a global audience.

In this book, I have shared my personal stories and have also added what in my honest opinion could be seen as lessons to learn from each story. My principal motivation is that these stories will help my readers reduce conflict, forge better relationships, and generally build a better world. My sincerest desire is that nobody will repeat my mistakes. That's why I have bared it all.

The world is like a school. We keep learning. I therefore have a strong conviction that my stories will continue, because I will certainly have more *Engaging Encounters* to experience and share in the future. Until then, please revisit the stories you just read, learn from them, and share your own unique stories. Together, we can and will heal the world and make this planet a better place.

God bless you!

Reflections and Group Study Lines

Chapter 1
Early Childhood Stories

1. What was your early childhood like? Reflect deeply on one or two remarkable events at home, school, or a place of worship that had a significant effect on your life. Share those significant stories with members of your group.
2. If you have deep painful stories from your childhood, do you still hurt from the experience? If yes, this is the time to let go. Forgive those who hurt you in your family, school, and places of worship. If you can reach those individuals, arrange a call. This is an opportunity for healing.
3. What are some remarkable personal lessons you've taken from your own stories? Have you really learned from them? Have you repeated the same mistakes? Share your lessons with other group members and receive feedback from them.

Chapter 2
Campus Stories

1. Life in the university offers opportunities for young adults to explore the world, make mistakes, and take personal responsibility for their actions. Can you share any key

decisions and actions you took while in university or a post–high school educational institution? Share with your group members.

2. What were the consequences of those actions you took? If you had a second chance to make those decisions, would your actions be different? Share with your group.

3. Consider the friends you made and the associations you belonged to then. Did they add value to your life or did they distract you from the main purpose of your life in school? Will you encourage your children or grandchildren to do the same?

4. Do you regret some of those decisions, especially as related to their impact on your life today? If you do, please forgive yourself. You made decisions based on what you knew then. You are wiser, older, and smarter now. This is a new you. Let that burden of guilt go. Many people made mistakes growing up. You are not alone. You will discover that you will make accelerated progress as the weight of that regret is lifted. Lift it now, and laugh out loud.

Chapter 3
Youth Life Encounters

1. We all had our firsts upon graduation: first car, first job, first apartment, first home. We were quite often not tutored on approaching these engagements. We had youthful exuberance. As you reflect on these, which experience stands out? Share with your group.

2. Recollect beautiful experiences you had as a youth—I mean, those experiences that gave you a sense of accomplishment and put a smile on your face, the ones you could repeat over and over. Share a key experience with your group. Laugh together and inspire one another

3. Are there some actions or projects you executed as a youth that you are still benefiting from today? For example, are you still married to the love of your youth? Celebrate that love. Are you still enjoying the home you purchased? Do you still miss your first car, even though you now have a better model? If the answer is yes, it means you were a near-genius as a youth. It means you should celebrate yourself. Share one of these stories and ask your group study members to rejoice with you.

Chapter 4
Marital Stories

1. For the sharing of stories, the group should be split between married and singles. Married members should share their failed and successful courtship experiences. Singles should share their active courtship experiences. Married members can provide counsel based on their experiences.
2. Let's talk about marriage. Can any member of the group share fears or phobia about marriage? Can anyone reflect on the marriage experiences of their parents? Do you have close friends or relatives who are happily married? Do you know of a model marriage you want to copy? What do you think makes marriage work? Do you know of marriages that have failed? Why do you think they failed? What can you do to ensure that your marriage never fails?
3. Let's project into the future. Paint a picture of you and your spouse on your twenty-fifth, fiftieth, and seventy-fifth wedding anniversaries. How beautiful is the picture? Do you see yourself playing with your great-grandchildren? Do you see yourself attending the wedding of a grandson or granddaughter along with your spouse?

Chapter 5
Parenting Stories

1. If you are already a parent, congratulations. You have literally seen it all. Giving birth, nursing a baby, and nurturing that child to adulthood has financial and emotional costs. You may have had to hold down many jobs and endured sleepless nights to succeed at this unending assignment called parenting. In your group study, let all parents give high-fives to one another. You've accomplished monumental tasks.

2. Reflect on some decisions you've made on behalf of your children. You decided who their father would be if you are a woman and who their mother would be if you are a man. You chose schools for them. You chose places of worship. All your input into the process of their growth has led to the final product you see now. You are also a final product of your parents' molding process. Do you feel they did a good job with you? If yes, explain why to your group. Then call your parents and give them some appreciation. If you feel proud of your children, appreciate yourself. Give each other one key reason why you feel so.

3. The work continues. Your children, God willing, will give you grandchildren. Do you already have grandchildren? Keep praying for them. If you are yet to have grandchildren, keep encouraging and supporting and praying for your adult children. Soon they will have their own children, which will make you a grandparent. Group members can share unique stories of guiding adult children and pray for one another.

Chapter 6
Career and Workplace Stories

1. Discuss job-search experiences. How did you secure your first job? How did you secure subsequent jobs? Let all group members share their unique stories.

2. If you have changed jobs, what motivated you to do so? Was it the take-home pay, the work environment, or the retirement benefits? Do you think you made smart decisions in changing jobs? Are you fulfilled? Share your experiences.

3. Are you running your own business? Are you fulfilled? How have you overcome challenges in becoming an owner-manager? Would you do it all over again if you had the chance? Share your experience with your group

4. How have you managed your bosses in the workplace? Are you tactical or strategic? Are you a reliable follower? Do you think your bosses and employers have respect for you? Do you think your staff performance evaluation reflects who you are? Is there room for improvement? Be honest with yourself. Share your fears and thoughts with your group study members and receive valuable feedback.

5. How have you managed your subordinate staff? If they were to honestly evaluate you on a scale of one to ten, where ten is excellent, where do you think your staff would rate you? Do you think you are a good role model? Do you think you are an excellent leader? Be honest with yourself. What area of leadership do you think you would need to work on to become a better leader in the workplace? Honestly share your fears and weaknesses with your group study members. Ask for honest feedback and counseling.

6. How have you related to your peers in the workplace? Are you loved or resented by your colleagues? Do your

peers truly look forward to working with you on team assignments, or do they merely tolerate you? Do you have inhibitions that restrain you from relating well with colleagues in the workplace? Does the workplace have a strong rumor mill that makes you very careful in relating with people?

7. How would you assess your self-esteem in the work environment? Are you knowledgeable? Do you have the skills necessary for your job? Do you feel sufficiently trained, or you are just tagging along? Are you confident in the workplace? Do you feel you are impactful? Are you producing results? Would your employer miss you if you were not on duty? Share your self-esteem personal evaluation with your study group members. Ask for honest counseling and feedback where you feel deficient.

8. How do you relate to external stakeholders? If you deal with vendors and suppliers, do they feel you have integrity and can deliver good results? If you relate with external customers who purchase your company's products and services, what's the customer feedback? Can you share your success stories or challenges with group study members?

9. What's your overall assessment of your workplace? Is it hostile? Is it a place of refuge or comfort? Does your heart skip when you remember you need to go back to work on a Monday morning? Share your fears and success stories.

10. Review your career choice. Are you happy doing what you are doing today? Would you do this same job even if you were not paid for it? Do you have career life satisfaction? If you are not happy in your current profession, it's not too late to change careers, no matter your age. Don't endure your profession; enjoy your profession. Share your thoughts with your group study members.

Chapter 7
Training Stories

1. When were you last trained for the job you are doing? Have you continued to obtain appropriate recertifications for your current job? Are you up-to-date with the current practices and policies of your profession? If you feel there is a gap, share it with your group. Share why you think that gap exists and seek feedback on how best to cover the gap.

2. Do you feel the need to seek a new skill to do something completely new? If you do, what is keeping you from acquiring that skill? Is it time or money? Share your challenge with your group and obtain advice.

3. Are you willing to sacrifice today so you can become sufficiently equipped to tackle tomorrow's challenges? How prepared are you to face future challenges?

4. Do you have sufficient financial and economic skills to manage your personal income, savings, and investment? Do you have enough knowledge to build personal wealth and live debt-free in old age? Share with your group. (Also, see my book *Financial Freedom: The Secrets of Debt-Free Living*.)

5. How much knowledge do you have in information technology to enable you to sufficiently cope in an IT world? Share your challenges, if any, with your group members.

6. Can you speak a major second language? What's stopping you from learning one? Do you know there are software applications that can teach you a second language? Share your inhibitions with your group and get feedback.

Chapter 8
Travels and Tours

1. How often do you travel within your country, either for business or for pleasure? Do you meet new people from diverse backgrounds when you travel? Please share your delightful experiences and shocking stories.

2. Have you experienced culture shocks during your trips? On foreign trips, have you been exposed to unusual experiences that brought fear or excitement? Did these experiences influence your life or break some mental walls? Do you understand the world better and see the world as a global village? Share your experiences.

3. What has been your experience with embassies in procuring visas and other travel documents? Has your visa application into any country ever been denied? What do you think was the reason, and what lessons have you learned? Share with your group.

About the Author

SIMON ARANONU holds a 1984 Bachelor's degree in Finance, and won the University foundation prize as the best graduating student in Finance. He is a Fellow of the Institute of Chartered Accountants and is also an Honorary member of the Chartered Institute of Bankers.

Simon attended a 1998 Advanced Management Program of Stanford University USA. He has also attended various business and leadership programs at Harvard Business school, University of Chicago, Wharton Business school and Kelloggs School of Business, Illinois, USA. He also trained at Cranfield University in the United Kingdom and Galilee Institute in Israel.

Simon started his banking career in 1987 with Continental Merchant Bank, a subsidiary of Chase Manhattan Bank (now JP Morgan Chase), has trained in Citibank and Chase Manhattan Bank, both in New York as well as at Mellon Bank, Philadelphia .

He benefited from the USAID sponsored "Best and Brightest African Bankers" program in the spring of 2000 in the United States.

Simon who has served as Executive Director in two other banks prior, is currently the Executive Director of Bank of Industry in Lagos Nigeria.

The author is at the same time senior Pastor in The Redeemed Christian Church of God (currently Assistant Pastor in charge of a Province). He has been happily married for over 30 years and is blessed with four biological children.

He has authored two other books already: SOLUTION CAPSULES and FINANCIAL FREEDOM.